An Introduction to
UTILITIES

An Introduction to
UTILITIES

by RON LANE

FIRST EDITION

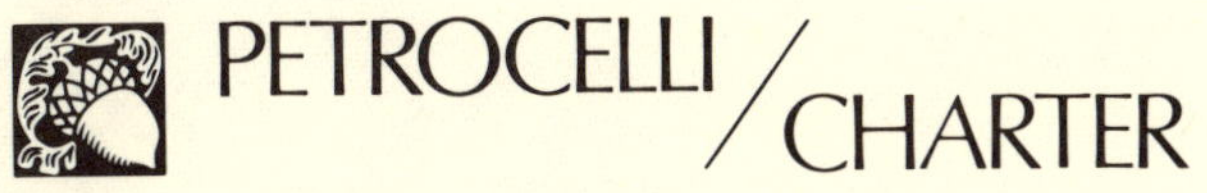

PETROCELLI/CHARTER

NEW YORK 1975

Library of Congress Cataloging in Publication Data

Lane, Ron.
    An introduction to utilities.

    1. Utilities (Computer programs) 2. IBM 360 (Computer)—Programming.
3. IBM 370 (Computer)—Programming. I. Title.
QA76.6.L333   001.6'424   75-19284
ISBN 0-88405-285-0

For Bill Shine

CONTENTS

PREFACE

An Introduction to Utilities is just that: an introduction. It describes the
Utilities used on IBM System/360 and System/370 computers using the OS
Operating System or the VS or VM Operating Systems.

It does not cover every function of every Utility, just the major, most common functions of the major Utilities. One reason the IBM Utilities manual is
so complicated and difficult for the beginner is that it has to cover all the possible functions of all the Utility programs. When you get to know how to use
them, you realize that 90 percent of the time (if not more), you do the same
functions, a small subset of all the available functions. You then say to yourself, "Perhaps it was a nice academic exercise to learn all the things that can
be done, even though I will never use them—but at the beginning, I wish I had
had a simple, straightforward manual that separated the chaff from the wheat,
so I could have quickly understood how to do the functions I almost always
use." Well, here is that manual.

Since it is directed toward the beginner, it also covers the basic JCL needed
to implement the Utilities. And it defines all the computer terms that one
needs to know to run the Utility programs. I tried to leave no stone left unturned, no term left undefined. Even a beginner to the computer field can
read this manual and be able to do the Utility functions he wants to do. And
almost anyone connected with a computer installation needs Utility programs done from time to time, if not on a regular basis.

Even those more familiar with the field will find the approach a clear way
of restating some of what they might already know. The manual summarizes
the knowledge into rules with examples, all listed in the appendix for convenience. The appendix also offers a simple way of finding which function of
which Utility you want when you have something specific to do. It refers the
reader to the rule and example, and perhaps the section of the manual referred
to, and there should be no trouble from there.

ACKNOWLEDGMENTS

The author's thanks go to Bob McCann for typing, illustrating, and pushing the original manuscript.

1 INTRODUCTION TO THE COMPUTER, DISK FILES, AND UTILITIES

Utilities are programs written by IBM to do various jobs that need to be done in a computer installation. They can tell you what's on disk packs and tapes, and move and change files in ways that are so common that to avoid each installation's having to write its own version of these utility programs, IBM wrote versions that we all use.

In this book we are going to describe the eight major Utilities: IEHLIST, IEHDASDR, IEBCOPY, IEHMOVE, IEBGENER, IEHPROGM, IEBPTPCH, and IEBUPDTE. It would be good now to describe briefly what each of them does, but before we can, we must describe some aspects of the computer, and the files and disk packs Utilities work with, in order to explain some of the terms we will be using in describing what the Utilities do.

THE COMPUTER, DISK PACKS, AND DISK FILES

The Computer

At the heart of all computers is the concept of the instruction. There are four main types of instructions: ADD, COMPARE, MOVE, and BRANCH. At the center of the computer itself is the processing unit, which has the circuitry to do what an instruction says should be done. The instructions themselves, kept in another part of the computer called main storage, are logically arranged to perform what is known as a program. One after another, about every millionth of a second, instructions are fetched from main storage and brought to the processing unit which performs the functions (ADD, COMPARE, MOVE, or BRANCH) described by the instructions.

Input/Output

The information that instructions work on also has to be in main storage, and since the size of main storage is limited, a large amount of information is

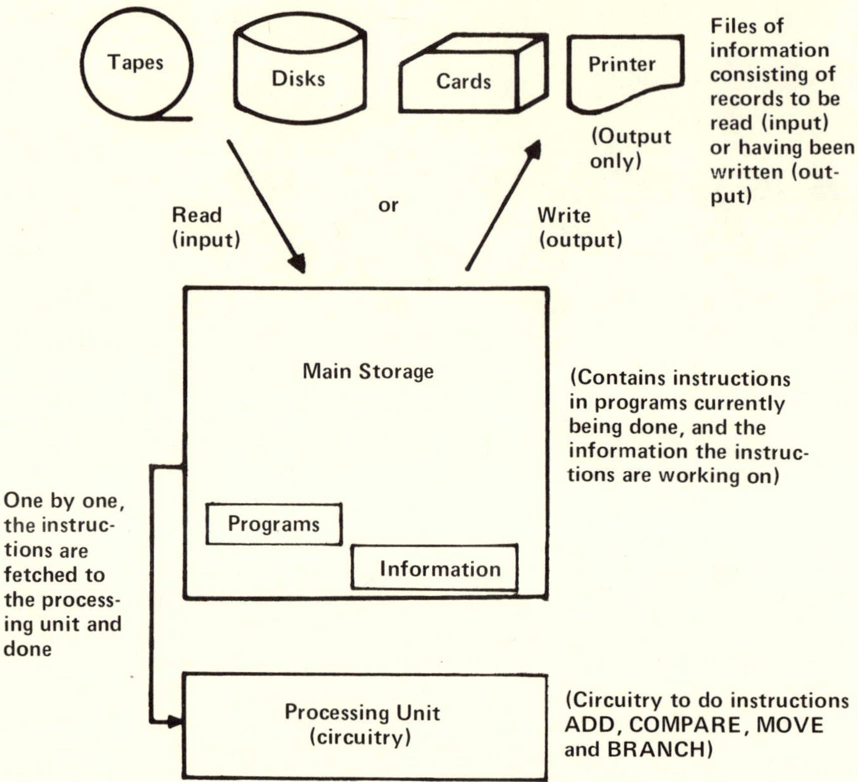

generally divided up into pieces, called records, and brought into main storage one at a time to be dealt with. All the records together make up what is known as a file, and the process of getting a record into main storage is called reading, or input. The results of programs are also usually divided into records; the process of getting them out of main storage is called writing, or output. There are four types of input/output devices where these files are kept: card reader/ punches, printers, tapes, and disks. They all can be read from or written to except the printer, which can only be written to.

The card reader/punch reads or punches thick paper cards that are usually divided into 80 columns, each of which can have holes punched in them representing information. The printer writes onto paper one line of information at a time, at a speed of about 400 to 2000 lines a minute. A tape is just like the ones used on a reel-to-reel tape recorder, and is generally about 2400 feet long.

The most complicated input/output device, and one that Utilities most often work with, is the disk.

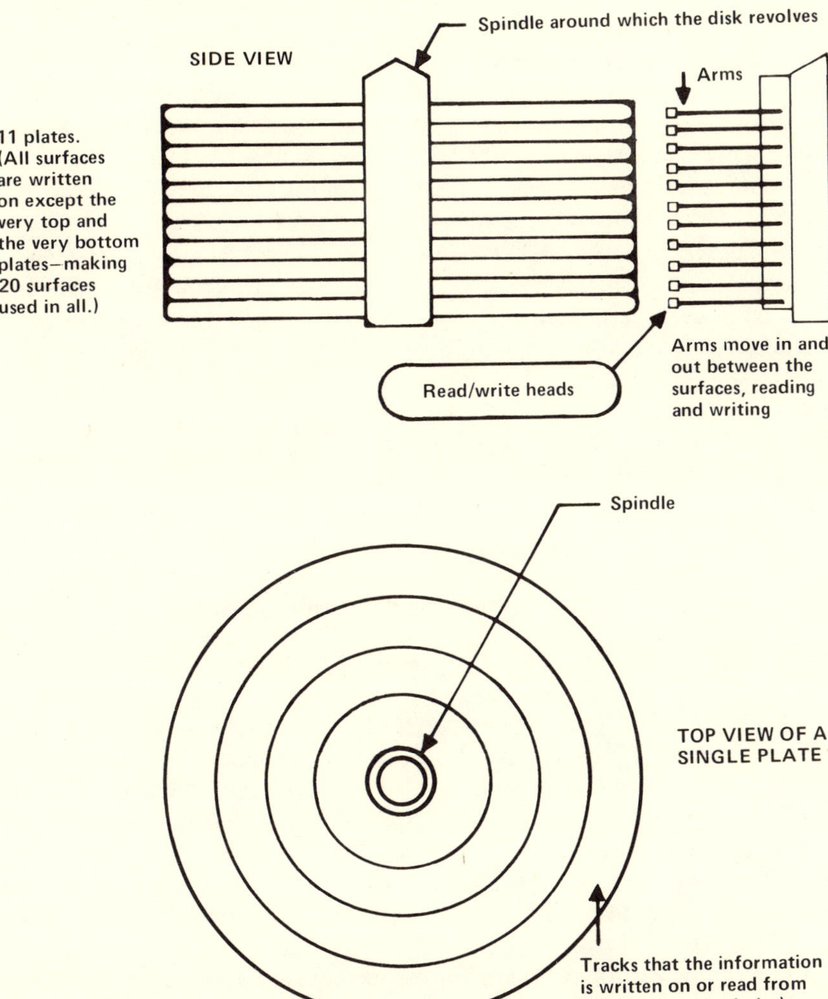

Fig. 1.1.　The disk pack (as an example here, 3330 is used).

Disk Packs

A disk pack* is made up of 11 round metal plates with a thick spindle running through the center of each of them, connecting them, so that they lie one on top of the other, each one about a half-inch away from the one be-

*The 3330 disk pack is used here as an example.

low. Both the top and bottom surfaces of each plate, except the very top and very bottom surfaces, are coated with a magnetic substance, so there are 20 magnetic surfaces in all. On each surface are 404 concentric circles, like waves coming out from the inner spindle; these circles are called tracks. When a disk is put on a disk drive and starts spinning around 3000 times a minute, arms come out from the walls of the disk drive and move between the surfaces, recording and sensing magnetic pulses on the tracks.

Initializing Disk Packs. When a disk comes from the factory, there is nothing recorded on the tracks. Before the disk can be used, a volume serial number must be put on the top surface's outermost track, as a means of identification. And second, an area must be reserved that can act as a center of information for all the files that will go on the disk. This area is called the *volume table of contents* (VTOC), for it describes the contents of the disk. When a file is then put on the disk, an entry is made in the VTOC describing it and pointing to where on the disk pack that file is. To delete a file from a disk pack, all that is necessary is that its entry in the VTOC be removed, and then the space it occupied is again considered available. This deletion is called *scratching* the file. The process of putting a volume serial number and a VTOC onto a new disk pack is called *initializing*, or analyzing, the disk pack.

Files

Partitioned Files. If you are looking for someone who is staying at a hotel, you check the hotel's directory to find out what room he is in. There is a common type of disk file organized the same way. At its beginning is a *directory*, and the rest of its disk space is divided up among its *members.* The directory lists the members in the file and says where they are. This type of file is called a *partitioned* data set, because the space is split up into partitions; sometimes it is called a *library* because it's similar to the way books in a library are located by a card catalog.

Compressing Partitioned Files. When a member moves into this file, he is assigned the next available room, and his name is added to the directory. When he moves out, his name is taken off the directory, but no one can then move into his room. You might say that the linen has to be changed first. After a lot of members move in and out, there may be no more rooms available, even though only a few of them are occupied. The file then has to be *compressed*, where all the rooms get cleaned, the current members are moved to the beginning of the file, and the rest of the rooms become available again.

Sequential Files. A second type of disk file is where there are no directories or members, just one block of information following another, starting at the beginning of the space it has and continuing to the end of the file. It is called a *sequential* file, and is simple and straightforward.

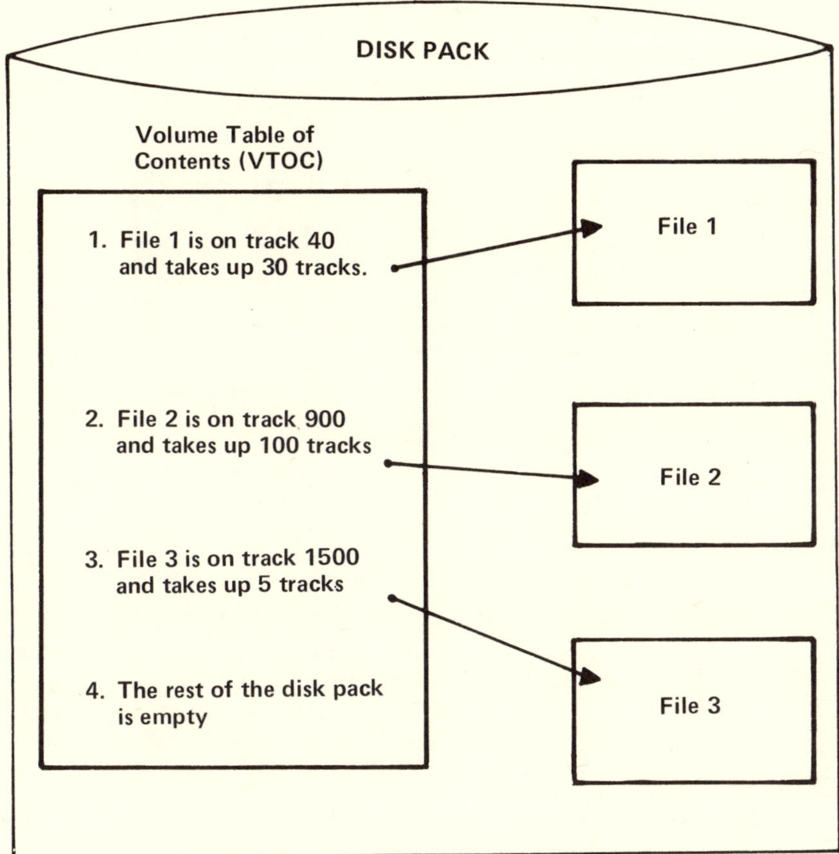

Fig. 1.2.   The volume table of contents (VTOC) points to where the files are
on the disk pack.

Dump/Restore. Sometimes the files on a disk pack are written on, changed, or deleted by mistake or in wrong ways. Since this could involve valuable, irreplaceable information, a safety measure would be to create an exact copy of all the files on a disk pack. What is most often done is that the pack as a whole is copied to a tape periodically. This is called *dumping* to a *backup* tape. Then if the files on the disk go bad, they can be wholly recovered by copying the information from the tape back onto the disk. This is called *restoring* the disk pack.

Two Types of Information on Disk Files. When a programmer writes a program, he punches onto IBM cards the words and numbers that describe what the program does. Before he can run the program, however, it first has to be

Partitioned File (Library)

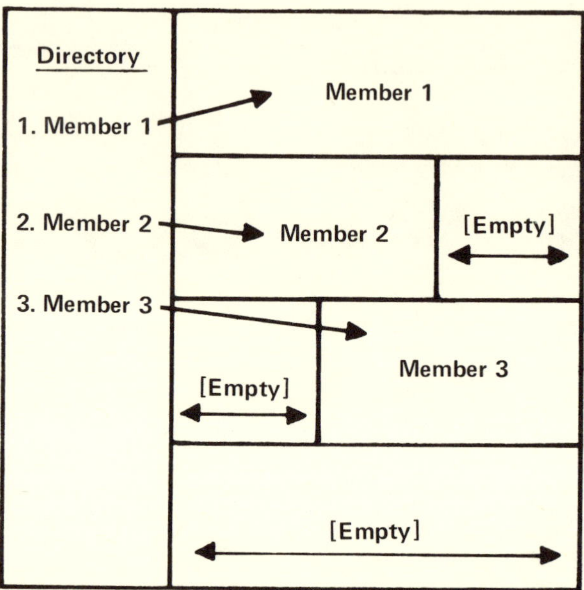

Fig. 1.3.   The directory is at the beginning of the file, and the rest of the file
is divided into areas where the members are. The directory points
to the location of the respective members. In this illustration, there
is an empty space between 2 and 3. This cannot be used until the
file is compressed, at which time 3 will be moved so that it immediately follows 2.

translated into a long series of numbers, which are instructions that the computer can understand. Some disk files are used to store such translated programs. But the information on the IBM cards themselves can also be stored in
disk files, and such files are said to contain card images because they consist
of the words and numbers just the way they looked on the cards themselves.
In other words, some disk files contain translated programs and other disk

Sequential File

Record 1	Record 2	Record 3	Record 4	. . . .	Last record

Fig. 1.4.   The records follow one right after the other, until the last record.

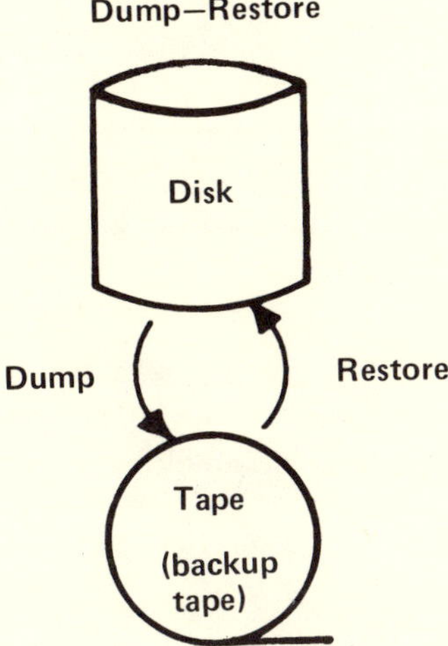

Fig. 1.5.   In a DUMP, the information on a disk is saved by placing it on a
backup tape. In RESTORE, the information is put back on the disk
from the tape.

files contain card images. One example of a card image file is SYS1.PROCLIB,
which contains frequently used Job Control Language.

Catalog. When you want to find a book in a library, you can look in a card
catalog under the name of the book to find where on the shelves the book is.
There is a similar kind of catalog on the system. It is a list of names of com-
monly used files, along with the volume serial number of the tape or disk
where those files are. A file whose name is on this list is said to be cataloged.

Online/Offline

The computer is a machine, a dumb, hulking mass of circuitry, memory,
and input/output devices. To run this machine, we load into its memory a
large IBM-written program called the Operating System, which then becomes
the thinking mind inside the physical computer. The Operating System com-
municates with the operator and oversees the jobs flowing through its system.
When the Operating System is first loaded, all the input/output devices are
within its field of awareness. When a job needs a device, like a disk or tape
drive, the Operating System finds one not being used and gives it to the job
for as long as the job uses it. All the devices that the Operating System has
available to it are considered on-line, or on its line of vision. The operator has
the ability to remove specific input/output devices from the Operating System's field of vision through the special VARY command. Then the device is

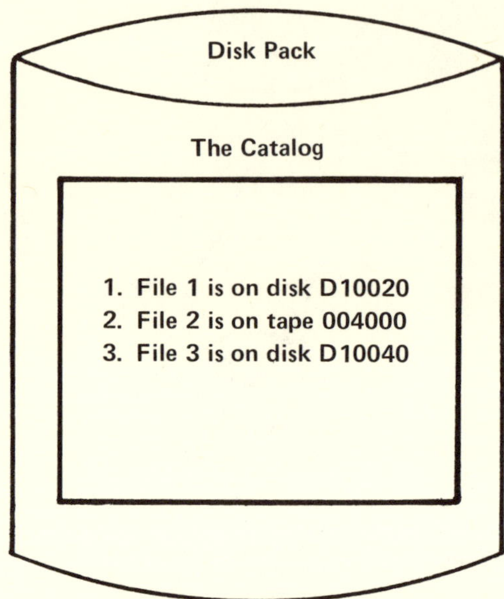

Fig. 1.6.   The catalog is just a list that gives the location of important files.

considered off-line, and though it is still physically attached to the computer, the Operating System no longer lends it to the jobs it runs. For instance, the operator can type in:

VARY   130,OFFLINE

Then the input/output device numbered 130 becomes offline, out of the Operating System's line of sight.

SUMMARY OF UTILITY FUNCTIONS

Now that you are familiar with all the terms we are going to use, we are able to describe what our eight Utilities do. First, what common functions need to be done? Basically there are three.
1. Look at, change, and move files.
2. Look at and change VTOCs, directories, and the catalog.
3. Initialize, back up, and restore disk packs.
The eight Utilities each have different functions.
1. IEHLIST lists volume table of contents, directories, and the catalog.
2. IEHDASDR initializes, dumps, and restores disk packs.

3. IEBGENER duplicates sequential files.

4. IEBCOPY copies and compresses partitioned files.

5. IEHMOVE backs up and restores partitioned files.

6. IEHPROGM catalogs, uncatalogs, scratches, and renames files and members.

7. IEBPTPCH prints out card image files.

8. IEBUPDTE updates partitioned card image files.

Following are each Utility's functions. Don't strain to remember it all—it will all become familiar to you as we go through each Utility in detail.

I. IEHLIST

    a. It can print out a disk pack's volume table of contents (VTOC), telling what files are on the disk pack.

    b. It can print out the directory of a partitioned file (library), telling the names of the members in that file.

    c. It can print out the catalog, which lists the names of the files that are cataloged and tells what disk and tapes they are on.

II. IEHDASDR

    a. It can initialize a new disk pack, which involves putting on the volume serial number and reserving space for the VTOC.

    b. It can search a disk pack for bad spots that are likely to cause input/output errors.

    c. It can change the volume serial number of a disk pack.

    d. It can print out the contents of specific tracks of a disk pack.

    e. It can create a backup tape by dumping the contents of a disk pack to tape.

    f. It can restore a disk pack by copying the information from a backup tape back onto a disk.

(The DASD in the name of the Utility stands for Direct Access Storage Device, which is the formal name for a disk pack.)

III. IEBGENER

It can copy one sequential file from one input/output device to another—from cards, tape, or disk to cards, printer, tape, or disk. Its most common functions are putting a card file on tape, copying one tape to another, and printing a tape. It is a "duplicating" utility for sequential files.

IV. IEBCOPY

    a. It can copy all the members of one partitioned file to another partitioned file.

    b. It can copy just some (or just one) of the members of one partitioned file to another partitioned file.

    c. It can compress a partitioned file, which cleans up the rooms, making those that are empty available for use again.

(IEBCOPY, as you can see, is used only with partitioned files.)

V. IEHMOVE

    a. It can unload (back up) a partitioned file to a backup tape.

    b. It can restore a partitioned file from a backup tape.

VI. IEHPROGM

    a. It can catalog a file, which means putting the name of the file on the catalog along with the number of the disk or tape it is on.

    b. It can uncatalog a file, which means taking its name off the catalog.

    c. It can scratch a file on a disk (also called deleting or erasing it), which means removing its entry from the VTOC and making space it occupied available for other files.

    d. It can scratch a member from a partitioned file, which means only removing its name from the directory of the file (its space does not become available until the file is compressed).

    e. It can rename a file on a disk, which means giving an entry in the VTOC a new name.

    f. It can rename a member of a partitioned file, which means giving the entry in the directory of the file a new name.

VII. IEBPTPCH

This Utility is used to print out (or punch out onto cards) the actual contents of a disk file in order to see the information that is in the file. This function can only be done for files that contain card images (not translated programs). If the file is partitioned, you can have it print out one, several, or all of the members. It can also duplicate a card deck, adding sequence numbers in columns 73–80 of a new card deck.

VIII. IEBUPDTE

IEBUPDTE is used to update (change) the information in a disk file. It only works for files that are partitioned (not sequential) and if the information to be updated is card images (not translated programs). For instance, it is used to add and change the little sets of Job Control Language which make up the members of SYS1.PROCLIB.

    a. It can add a whole new member of card images to the file, which means taking the information on some IBM cards and placing it in the file as a totally new member. You give this new member a name, which is put in the directory of the file.

    b. It can add new information to a member already in the file, which means taking new card images and putting them in the middle or at the end of the card images already there in the member.

    c. It can change the information already in a member, which means taking a new card image and writing the information on it right over an old card image already there in the member. The new line just replaces the old line.

    d. It can delete information from a member, taking away some card images and leaving the rest.

e. It can create an entirely new partitioned card image file, complete with new members.

Again:
1. IEHLIST lists volume table of contents, directories, and the catalog.
2. IEHDASDR initializes, dumps, and restores disk packs.
3. IEBGENER duplicates sequential files.
4. IEBCOPY copies and compresses partitioned files.
5. IEHMOVE backs up and restores partitioned files.
6. IEHPROGM catalogs, uncatalogs, scratches, and renames files and members.
7. IEBPTPCH prints out card image files.
8. IEBUPDTE updates partitioned card image files.

MAIN STORAGE REQUIREMENTS FOR THE UTILITIES

Each Utility requires a different amount of main storage to run in, to hold instructions and input/output areas. In the next chapter, we will see how you can ask for the amount of main storage your Utility will need. Now we will show how to figure out how much to ask for. But first, a few necessary terms.

K

The computer was made possible when it was realized that one could perform arithmetic and logical operations with a numbering system called binary, which uses only two numbers, 0 and 1, and that this could be done electronically by having the 0 be something that is *off* and the 1 be the same thing turned *on*.

All over the computer—in main storage, in the processing unit, even in the files themselves on the disks and tapes—are little things called bits, which are turned on and off to represent numbers, letters, and instructions. By convention, these bits are used in groups of eight, called bytes. And when we talk about main storage, there are usually so many bytes that for convenience we divide them into groups of about 1000 bytes each (1024 to be exact), and say that each group is equal to one K. In other words, 1K is equal to about 1000 bytes, 20K is equal to 20,000 bytes, and so on.

Buffers

Utility programs, like all programs, are made up of instructions that can only operate on information in main storage. Therefore, as mentioned before, files are divided into sections called records, which are read into main storage or written from main storage. These physical records into which the file is divided are also referred to as blocks.

While these blocks are in main storage, they occupy areas reserved for them, called *buffers*. The size of the main storage buffers needed for the blocks to be read into or written from is equal to the size of the blocks themselves.

The total main storage needed for a Utility program to run in is usually a combination of the size of the program itself (the instructions), plus the space needed for buffers. This total main storage requested is sometimes called the *region*.

Determining the Storage Requirements

So here are the main storage requirements for our eight Utilities. In our shorthand, B is the size (in bytes) of the largest block on any of the files that the Utility is working with. To get B, you need to know the size of the blocks on your files.

Don't be exact because you'll be adding a large "fudge factor" anyway.

IEHLIST	44K
IEHDASDR	52K
IEBGENER	14K + B
IEBCOPY	28K + 2B
IEHMOVE	16K + B
IEHPROGM	44K
IEBPTPCH	16K + B
IEBUPDTE	14K + 2B

After figuring this out, add about 4 to 6K, just to be on the safe side.

We will not include the REGION parameter in the examples in the following pages, because the correct region size so often depends on the file you are using.

QUESTIONS

1. What are the four main types of instructions?
2. What part of the computer actually does what the instructions say should be done?
3. *a.* Where does the processing unit fetch the instructions from?
    b. What is a logical series of instructions called?
4. About how long does it take for the processing unit to perform an instruction?
    a. A hundredth of a second.

     b. A thousandth of a second.

     c. A millionth of a second.

5. Where does information have to be in order for instructions to work on it?

6. Since the size of main storage is limited and can't contain all the information to be used by a program, the information is divided into pieces. What are these pieces called?

7. What is a collection of records called?

8. What are the two words that describe each of the following processes:
   a. Getting records into main storage from a file.
   b. Getting records out of main storage to a file to be kept for later use.

9. Reading and writing, then, are done mainly with four types of input/output devices. Name them.

10. *a.* How many round, metal plates are on a 3330 disk pack?
    b. How many surfaces are recorded on?
    c. Which two surfaces are not recorded on?

11. What is the name for the "grooves" in which the disk records and reads its information on the disk pack?

12. *a.* What two things must be put on a disk pack before it is used?
    b. What is the process of putting them on called?

13. When a file is put on a disk pack, where is an entry describing the file put?

14. *a.* What is always at the beginning of a partitioned file?
    b. What does it contain?

15. *a.* When a member is "moved out" of a partitioned file, can the space it occupied be reused immediately if needed?
    b. What has to be done first to make it available?

16. A disk can be dumped to a backup tape for safety; what is the process called of putting the information from the backup tape back onto the disk pack?

17. Does SYS1.PROCLIB, which contains frequently used JCL, contain translated programs or card images?

18. What type of device can't the Operating System lend to the jobs it runs?

19. What three things can IEHLIST list out for you?

20. What type of device does IEHDASDR work with?

21. What two things can IEHPROGM do to the following:
    a. The catalog.
    b. A volume table of contents.
    c. A directory of a partitioned file.

22. What do the letters PTPCH in IEBPTPCH stand for?

23. Which of the following Utilities work with partitioned files, and which work with sequential files?
    a. IEBCOPY.

        b. IEBGENER.

        c. IEBUPDTE.

24. What numbering system has just the two numbers 0 and 1?
25. How many bits are there in a byte?
26. How many bytes are there in one K of main storage?
27. If a file is divided into blocks of information each 800 bytes long, how big must a main storage buffer be to accommodate such a file?
28. The amount of main storage needed to run a Utility program is usually a combination of what two factors?

2 JCL

Let's say we have a job to do that we think can be done by a Utility program. We can look through the appendix of this book, which provides a helpful method of selecting which Utility to use, reading the description of what each program does until we find the one we want. Often the names are a clue, such as IEHLIST and IEBCOPY (all Utilities begin with either IEH or IEB—an IBM naming convention).

The Utility programs themselves are on a system disk pack, and once we select the one we want, we then want to get it into main storage and have it do what we tell it. This is done with Job Control Language (JCL), so let's learn the JCL needed to run Utilities.

INTRODUCTION

JCL cards begin with a // in columns 1 and 2 to identify them as JCL cards. The rest of the card is always divided into a beginning, a middle, and an end; each part is separated by at least one blank. The beginning, always starting in column 3, right after the //, is the name of the card, which can be up to eight letters (and/or numbers), but must start with a letter. The middle tells which of the three kinds of JCL cards (JOB, EXEC, or DD) this one is. We will cover more on this a little later. The end is a combination of all kinds of parameters and information that can go on that kind of card. Each parameter is separated by a comma (no blanks), and the last parameter is followed by a blank, indicating the end of the card. Again, the three parts must have at least one blank separating them from each other.

THE JOB CARD

The work that you want done by the computer that you describe with JCL is called a job (Job Control Language). Every job must begin with a JOB card. Let's look at a typical JOB card:

```
Beginning    Middle              End
//LISTVTOC    JOB    (accnt),NAME,MSGLEVEL=(1,1)
```

1. It begins with a // in columns 1 and 2, just like all JCL cards.
2. The // is immediately followed in column 3 (no blank is allowed after the //) by the name of the JOB card. Notice it is eight letters long, the maximum length for a name. This name on the JOB card becomes the name of the entire job. The system uses this name whenever it refers to this job. This is the name that is used to cancel, display, or release a job. It is the name that comes out in big block letters on the printout.
3. After at least one blank, the letters JOB appear identifying this card as a JOB card.
4. The "end" of the JOB card has three pieces of information, each separated by a comma (not a blank).
   a. First comes a field of accounting information. It is often used for billing purposes. This is extremely variable from installation to installation, so to indicate its presence we will just put the word "accnt" in parenthesis. Find out what your installation requires and use that instead.
   b. The name of the programmer or department can be longer than eight characters and can have periods in it; however, no blanks or commas. It can be any name.
   c. A field that says that all JCL is to be printed out—MSGLEVEL=(1,1). These three fields have to be in this order. Just remember them and put them down the same way on every JOB card

THE EXEC CARD

The EXEC card always immediately follows the JOB card. Its main function is to specify which of the Utility programs you want executed. For example:

```
//STEP1  EXEC  PGM=IEHLIST,REGION=50K
```

As with all JCL cards, there is a // in columns 1 and 2.
1. The "beginning" of the EXEC card, right after the //, is the name of this card. It must follow the naming rules of being not more than eight characters long and starting with a letter. It is not important, and can even be left out. In our examples, all EXEC cards are arbitrarily named STEP1.
2. Then, following at least one blank, are the four letters EXEC, to identify this card as an Execute Card.

3. After that comes the main part of the card, the name of the program. Just put the PGM= and the name of the Utility program that you want run.
4. The last parameter, REGION=, is not absolutely required—the job will run without it—but it is put in by most careful programmers. It indicates how much main storage your Utility will need to run in. (How to determine this amount was discussed in the previous chapter.) Just say REGION= followed by the amount of main storage you want, and then the letter K. For example, REGION=50K asks for 50,000 bytes of main storage. If you leave out this parameter, a standard size is assigned, which is usually more than you need.

So far we've given a name to the job and said which program we want run. All Utility programs read and write some kind of files, at least to get information to work with (input) and to tell us what it has done (output). These files can be on any of the four types of input/output devices: card readers, printers, disks, and tapes. Each file that a program uses has to be described on the third, last, and most involved JCL card, called the DD card (DD stands for data definition).

THE DD CARD

The DD cards follow immediately after the EXEC card, and there is one for each file. Again, let's look at an example:

```
//DISK   DD   UNIT=3330,VOL=SER=D10040,DISP=OLD
```

1. After the usual // in columns 1 and 2, there comes the name of the DD card, called the DD name, which must follow the normal naming rules of being eight or less characters, the first of which must be a letter. Sometimes Utilities require specific DD names for their DD cards, and here are the basic four:
   a. SYSPRINT. A DD card with this name is required by every Utility. It is the printout, where the Utility gives you the information you want and/or tells you if it has completed successfully.
   b. SYSIN. Again, a DD card with this name is required by every Utility. The SYSIN file is the control card input, which we will come to later.
   c. SYSUT1. Required by only some Utilities. When it is used, it refers to the input file.
   d. SYSUT2. Required by only some Utilities, usually in conjunction with the SYSUT1 DD name. It refers to the output file.

We will see how these four DD names are used with the specific Utilities later. When a specific DD name is not required, you can use any name. In our examples, the DD names DISK and TAPE are arbitrarily used for disk and tape files, respectively. Each DD card must have a different name.

2. After the DD name, and separated from it by at least one blank, are the two letters DD, identifying this as a DD card.

3. The rest of the DD card contains the parameters that describe the file. We will take the parameters required for each of the four kinds of input/output devices separately.

    a. Printer. If you want a printer, just say SYSOUT=A. What this does is spool your printed output onto a disk spool pack and have it printed when the job ends. SYSOUT stands for system output. Every Utility requires a DD card that looks exactly like this:

```
//SYSPRINT  DD  SYSOUT=A
```

    b. Card reader. To define a card file, just put an * and follow the DD card with the card file itself. For example, all Utilities require a DD card that looks exactly like this:

```
//SYSIN  DD  *
```

This is immediately followed by a control card (written by you) that the Utility will read in order to find out what it is supposed to do.

    c. Card punch. The other half of the card reader is the card punch, and it is used, predictably enough, to punch out cards. It can only be used as an output device, just as the card reader can only be used as an input device. If you want your output to be punched on cards, just say:

```
SYSOUT=B
```

THE PARAMETERS FOR DISKS AND TAPES

Now comes the most involved and interesting part, the key to JCL—what is put to the right of the letters DD for disks and tapes. There are six parameters used in a variety of combinations: UNIT, VOL=SER, DISP, DSN, LABEL, and SPACE.

First, we'll go through the meanings of each of these parameters, and then describe how they're used for disk and tapes.

1. UNIT defines the kind of device. For disk it can be UNIT=2314, 2311, or 3330, depending on the type of disk you are using. For tape, depending on the type of tape it is, it can be UNIT=2400, 2400-1, 2400-2, 2400-3, or 2400-4 for the 2400 series—or 3400, 3400-1, 3400-2, 3400-3, or 3400-4 for the 3400 series. For drum, it can be UNIT=2301, 2303, or 2305, again depending on the type of drum. For simplicity's sake, in our examples we will assume an imagin-

ary installation using 3330 disks, 3400-3 tapes, and 2305 drums. But you better check what devices your installation has before you fill out your UNIT parameters for disk and tapes.

Sometimes an installation may refer to disks or tapes by the installation's own names, instead of using the above numbers. You should check with your installation and use whatever names or numbers that it requires.

2. VOL=SER is the volume serial number, which is put on the beginning of a disk or tape when it is labeled, and is used from then on to identify it. In the examples, hypothetical disk D10040 is used so the DD cards refer to it with VOL=SER=D10040; the hypothetical tape is 004000, referred to by VOL=SER=004000. (Notice that all six digits must be used—VOL=SER=4000 won't do.)

3. DISP stands for disposition. It answers two questions about the file:
    a. Does it exist before the job is run? If we are creating the file, we say it is NEW. If it already exists, we say it is OLD.
    b. Do we want to keep the file after the job is run? If yes, we say KEEP. If no, we say DELETE.

Each question is answered separately, the first one first, the second one second, separated by a comma and enclosed by parentheses.

For example, for a file we want to keep that already exists, we say DISP=(OLD,KEEP). If we create it and want to keep it, we say DISP=(NEW,KEEP). If it's a temporary work space file, we'd say DISP=(NEW,DELETE) if we won't need it anymore, and so on.

A very important point must be made here. When JCL was first developed, it was a rule that a file could be used by only one person at a time. Then somewhere along the line, someone thought: when reading from a disk file, there's no harm in allowing many people to read from that disk file at the same time. As long as no one is changing the file (writing to it), why make each person wait in line to use it? Thus was born SHR, which means, "The file already exists, I am not changing it, and anyone can use it at the same time I do." So you can say DISP=(SHR, ...) instead of DISP=(OLD, ...), and allow the file to be shared.

This is such an important point because to use OLD when you can use SHR is to make everyone unnecessarily wait in line for a file they could be sharing. This can sometimes slow the system down considerably. So from here on in, we will always use SHR in the DISP parameter for a disk file unless we are changing the contents of the disk file, in which case we must lock out others while we are making the change.

4. DSNAME. When a tape or disk file is created, you give it a name, called a data set name (DSNAME), so that when you want to read it in the future, you can specify its name. For instance, a disk pack could contain many files, so you have to give the DSNAME of the file you want so it can be located. An example:

DSNAME=TAPEFILE. You can also use the abbreviation, and just say
DSN=TAPEFILE.

5. LABEL applies to tapes. A tape fresh from the factory usually has a
label put at its beginning specifying its volume serial number. This is done
with the Utility program IEHINITT; when files are then written on it, the
tape looks like this:

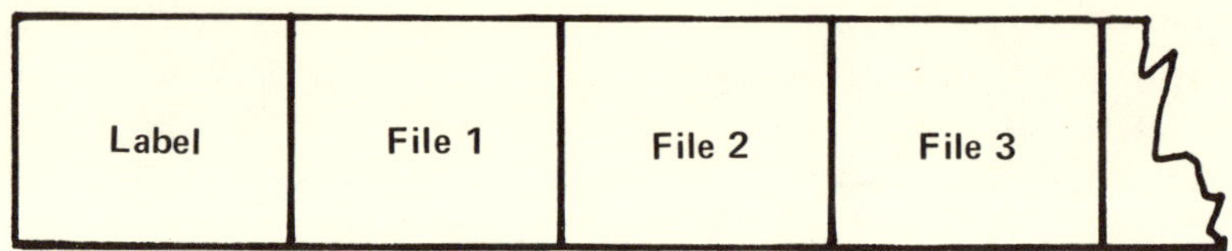

If, however, the tape is left unlabeled and files are written on it, it would look
like this:

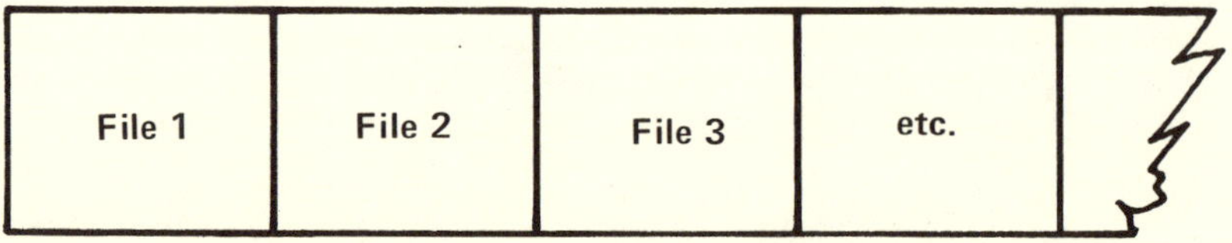

The LABEL parameter, again, answers two questions:
  a. What is the number of the file on the tape that we want to read or
     write? We put 1 for the first file, 2 for the second file, etc.
  b. Does the tape have a label? If yes, we put SL for standard labels. If no,
     we put NL for no labels.
If we want all label processing bypassed, we say BLP (bypass label processing).
The only difference between NL and BLP is that, with NL, labeled tapes will not
be accepted; with BLP, any tape is accepted. To position yourself at the first
file on a labeled tape (which is usually the case), say LABEL=(1,SL), the second
file on a labeled tape is LABEL=(2,SL), and the first file on a nonlabeled tape
is LABEL=(1,NL), and so on.

6. SPACE is only used when you are creating a file on a disk, and it specifies how big you want the file to be. There are three things to tell it:
  a. Whether you are specifying the size in tracks or cylinders. For example,
     on a 3330, there are 7676 tracks, or 404 cylinders; that is, there are 19
     tracks per cylinder. If you are going to specify the size in tracks, say
     TRK; if in cylinders, say CYL.
  b. The first number is the initial size of the file.
  c. The second number is how much extra space to give it if it runs out of
     room while you are writing on it. If the space keeps on filling up, this

secondary quantity is added on up to 15 times; if it still needs more
space, the job will end with a B37 completion code. This second number can be left out, and then if the *initial* size is used up, the job will
end with a D37 completion code.

The syntax is interesting. SPACE=(TRK,8) means Give me eight tracks, but no
more. SPACE (CYL,8) means Give me eight cylinders, but no more.

SPACE=(TRK,(8,2)) means Give me eight tracks initially, but if while writing
I run out of space, tack on another two tracks, and if again I run out, give me
another two tracks. If, after tacking on these two-track quantities 15 times
(for a total of 38 tracks in all), I still need more, make me end with a B37
completion code.

SOME NEW TERMS

Now we have gone over the six parameters: DSNAME, UNIT, VOL=SER,
DISP, LABEL, and SPACE. But not all six are used to describe every type of file.
Before enumerating some basic rules describing when to use which ones, it is
necessary to introduce some new terms:

1. DEFAULT. If someone tells you he flew to California, you assume,
though he doesn't explicitly say so, that he went by airplane. In JCL, in the
same way, some parameters can be left out, and the system will just assume a
value that is the most common for that parameter. That value is called the default for that parameter.

2. TEMPORARY. Some programs need work space (usually on disk) to
hold information while the program is running. But then, when the program
ends, the work space is no longer needed and can be deleted (erased). A file
that is created and then deleted by the same job is called a temporary file.

3. SCRATCH TAPES and SCRATCH PACKS. When you want to create a
new file on tape, and you don't care which tape it goes on, the system will
have mounted an unused tape for you, which you can then write on. Such a
tape is called a scratch tape. If you want to create a new file on disk, and you
don't care which disk it goes on, the system will grab some unused space for
you on an available disk pack. Such a disk pack is called a scratch pack. There
may be installation standards regarding the use of these scratch tapes or disks.
You should check with your installation.

THE SEVEN BASIC RULES

1. *The default for the* LABEL *parameter* is LABEL=(1,SL).   If you leave out
the LABEL parameter, the system assumes that the file is the first file on tape
and that the tape is labeled. Since this is usually the case, the LABEL parameter

is seldom needed—except of course, when the file is not the first on the tape or, rarely, when the tape is not labeled.

2. *The* SPACE *parameter is needed only when you are creating a new file on disk.*   If the file already exists (OLD, i.e., the file already has space) or if it is on tape, the SPACE parameter is not needed (must not be used).

3. *If you say* DISP=OLD, *the system assumes you mean* DISP=(OLD,KEEP), *and if you say* DISP-SHR, *the system assumes you mean* DISP=(SHR,KEEP). This is because most jobs that use old files do not delete them.

4. *The full default for the* DISP *parameters is* DISP=(NEW,DELETE).   If you leave out the DISP parameter entirely, the system assumes your file is NEW and will not be needed after the job ends, so it can be deleted. This is mainly true for temporary files.

5. When creating a new file on tape or disk, and it doesn't matter which tape or disk the file goes on, *leave out the* VOL=SER *parameter and the system will have mounted for you a scratch tape or get space on a scratch pack.*

6. *If the file you are using is cataloged, you can leave out the* UNIT *and* VOL=SER *parameters.*   The system will then look in the catalog for the file's unit type and volume serial number.

7. Many Utilities refer to a whole disk pack, not just one file on the disk pack. *If you want to refer to a whole disk pack, leave out the* DSNAME *parameter.*

THE EIGHT TYPES OF FILES

There are only eight possible types of files. Here are the parameters you need for each of them.

1. *Old file on disk (not cataloged)*

DSNAME, UNIT, VOL=SER, DISP=OLD (or SHR)

SPACE is not needed because the file already exists and has the space it needs. LABEL is not needed for disk packs.

2. *Old file on disk (cataloged)*

DSNAME, DISP=OLD (or SHR)

SPACE and LABEL are not needed for the same reason as above. UNIT and VOL=SER information is obtained from the catalog.

3. *Old file on tape (not cataloged)*

DSNAME, UNIT, VOL=SER, DISP=OLD

LABEL could be used if the label characteristics are unusual. SPACE is not used for tapes.

4. *Old file on tape (cataloged)*

DSNAME, DISP=OLD

Again, LABEL could be used in unusual cases, and SPACE is not needed for tapes. The UNIT and VOL=SER information is obtained from the catalog.

5. *New file on disk*

DSNAME, UNIT, DISP=(NEW,KEEP), SPACE

In this case, VOL=SER could be put in, naming a specific disk you want the file to go on. If left out, a scratch pack will be used. LABEL is not needed for disks.

6. *New file on tape*

DSNAME, UNIT, DISP=(NEW,KEEP)

Again, you can name a specific volume with VOL=SER, but usually a scratch tape is good enough. LABEL could be used for unusual label characteristics. SPACE is not needed for tapes.

7. *Temporary file on disk*

UNIT, SPACE

This looks surprising, because almost all the parameters are left out. The DSNAME can be left out because in this case the system will create its own temporary name. VOL=SER is left out so that a scratch pack will be used. DISP can be left out because it defaults to DISP=(NEW,DELETE), which is the case here. LABEL is only used for tapes.

8. *A whole disk pack*

UNIT, VOL=SER, DISP=OLD (or SHR)

This is for those cases when the Utility wants to look at a whole disk and not just one file on it. DSNAME is left out because the whole pack, and no particular file, is being used. SPACE is not needed because no new file is being created. LABEL is only needed for tapes.

From the above cases, it is clear that the basic four parameters are DSNAME, UNIT, VOL=SER, and DISP, since SPACE and LABEL are used much less often. And when you have to make up a DD card for a file, just ask yourself the following questions:

    a. Is the file on disk or tape?
    b. Is it new, old, or temporary?
    c. Is it cataloged?

CONTINUATION OF JCL CARDS

Sometimes you'll find that a JCL card has too many parameters to fit all on one card. In that case, it can be continued onto another card if certain rules are followed: The last parameter on the first card cannot go beyond column 70, and must be followed by a comma indicating that more parameters are to come on another card. The second card must have a // in columns 1 and 2, and then, after at least one blank, the rest of the parameters. These continuation parameters may begin in any column between 3 and 16, but not after column 16.

Now you should have enough understanding of Job Control Language to write the JCL needed to use Utilities. So let's go on to the Utilities themselves.

QUESTIONS

1. With what two letters do the names of all Utilities begin?
2. What is in the first two columns of every JCL card?
3. What are the three main types of JCL cards?
4. On which JCL card do you put the name of the Utility program you want to use? As part of what parameter?
5. *a.* As part of what parameter do you specify how much main storage your program needs to run?
   b. How would you use this parameter to ask for 50,000 bytes?
   c. On what JCL card does this parameter go?
6. What are the four main types of input/output devices?
7. What do the letters DD stand for?
8. Every JCL card has a name.
   a. Where is it put on the card?
   b. How many characters can it have?
9. Does the SYSUT2 DD card describe the input file or the output file?
10. What DD card parameter do you use to say that you want your output to go to the printer?
11. What DD card parameter do you use to say that you want your output punched out on cards?
12. What are the six parameters that can go on a DD card for disks and tapes?
13. *a.* What type of unit is a 3400-3?
    b. A 3330?
14. How would you use the DISP parameter to say the following:
    a. "I'm creating the file now, and I want it to be kept after the job ends."
    b. "The file already exists (my job is not creating it), I want to use it ex-

clusively, and when my job ends, no one will be needing it anymore, so
get rid of it."
   c. "The file already exists, other people can use it at the same time I do,
and I'm going to need it in the future."

15. If five people are running jobs at the same time, using the same file, and
they all use SHR in their DISP parameter to refer to the file, can they all
run at the same time?

16. When is the only time you should use OLD in the DISP parameter? (Select one.)
   a. When you are using more than one file.
   b. When you are reading from the file.
   c. When you are writing to the file (changing its contents).

17. What three letters always follow VOL=?

18. What is the abbreviation for DSNAME?

19. How would you use the LABEL parameter to say the following:
   a. "Position me at the beginning of the first file of a labeled tape."
   b. "Position me at the beginning of the second file of an unlabeled tape."

20. How would you use the SPACE parameter to say the following:
   a. "Give me 30 cylinders of disk space, but no more."
   b. "Give me 20 tracks of disk space, and if it runs out, keep giving me
groups of 10 more tracks."

21. What parameter is the default for:
   a. LABEL?
   b. DISP?

22. Is the SPACE parameter needed to describe the following files?
   a. An old file on disk.
   b. An old file on tape.
   c. A new file on disk.
   d. A new file on tape.

23. *a.* If your file is cataloged, what two parameters can be left out?
   b. Where will that information then be obtained?

24. If you leave out the VOL=SER parameter for a file you are creating on
disk, how does the system know which disk to put the file on?

25. What parameters are needed to describe the following:
   a. An old file on tape (not cataloged).
   b. An old file on disk (cataloged).
   c. A new file on disk.
   d. A temporary file on disk.
   e. A whole disk pack.

26. Of the six parameters that go on DD cards for disk and tape, which two
are used less often than the others?

3 THE CONTROL CARD

FRAMEWORK OF JCL

Let's say you think there may be a Utility that can accomplish a task for you.
First, look over the list of Utilities and what they do (use the appendix). If
you find one that fits, your next problem is to punch out the cards that, when
read into the computer, will get that Utility to do what you want.

The set of cards that you will need has the same general information for
every Utility. Here is the skeleton:

```
//JOBNAME   JOB    (accnt),NAME,MSGLEVEL=(1,1)
//STEP1     EXEC  PGM= (1)
//SYSPRINT  DD     SYSOUT=A
           (2)
//SYSIN     DD     *
           (3)
/*
//
```

This skeleton of Job Control Language is the same for every Utility. You always need these six cards, and they are always exactly the same. So memorize
them and the order they're in. And as you can see, there are three things that
you have to fill into this skeleton, depending on which function of which
Utility you want to use.

The first is easy. Just put here the name of the Utility that you want to
use. If you chose to use IEHLIST, your second card would look like this:

```
//STEP1   EXEC   PGM=IEHLIST
```

Numbers (2) and (3) are not so easy, for they differ with each function of
each Utility. They are the heart of learning how to use the Utilities, and they
will become our focus of attention from now on.

In the place marked (2) are put the DD cards for the disk and tape files that the Utility will use. As we go through each Utility, we will describe what DD cards are required, and when. The beginning section on JCL will then come in handy. In the place marked (3), right after the SYSIN DD card, you put what is called the control card. This is where you put the information that tells the Utility what to do. It is not JCL and has its own format, which we will now describe.

THE CONTROL CARD

Column 1 must be blank. In column 2, there is placed an action word that tells the Utility what action to take. (IEBUPDTE is the lone exception to this rule, having a ./ in columns 1 and 2 of its control cards; its action words start in column 4. But we'll come to that later.) Following is a list of all the action words for each Utility. We'll go over them in detail later, but you can see how they can tell the Utility which of its various functions to perform.

Utility	*Action Words*
IEHLIST:	LISTVTOC, LISTPDS, LISTCTLG
IEHDASDR:	ANALYZE, DUMP, RESTORE, LABEL
IEBGENER:	(has no action words)
IEBCOPY:	COPY, SELECT, EXCLUDE
IEHMOVE:	COPY
IEHPROGM:	CATLG, UNCATLG, SCRATCH, RENAME
IEBUPDTE:	CHANGE, ADD, NUMBER, DELETE, ENDUP
IEBPTPCH:	PRINT, RECORD, MEMBER, PUNCH

The action word is followed by a blank and then a series of parameters that describes to what and in what way the action is to be done. Learning these parameters will expand your computer vocabulary by 34 words. Don't be frightened by the number of new terms, because there's a logic to when they're used. No Utility uses more than six of them at a time, and with use it will become second nature to you which terms go with each action. We list these terms in four different ways, just so they will look familiar to you when you learn what they mean in the discussion of the individual Utilities.

First, we'll just list all 34 of them in alphabetical order. Just scan the list to get a feel for them:

BEGIN=	DSNAME=	FORMAT
CDINCR=	END=	FROM=
CDSEQ=	EXTENT=	FROMDD=
CVOL=	FIELD=	INCR=

INDD=   NEW1=   SEQ2=
LIST=ALL   OUTDD=   TO=
MAXFLDS=   PASSES=   TODD=
MAXNAME=   PDS=   TYPORG=PO
MEMBER=   PURGE   UPDATE=INPLACE
NAME=   PURGE=YES   VOL=
NEWNAME=   SEQ1=   VTOC
NEWVOLID=

In some cases, the words themselves give a clue as to what they might be
used for to describe—such as DSNAME, MEMBER, and VTOC. In the following
list of which Utilities use which words, you may notice that a few words are
used by more than one Utility, such as DSNAME and VOL. Again, just go over
them quickly; we'll consider them in greater detail later.

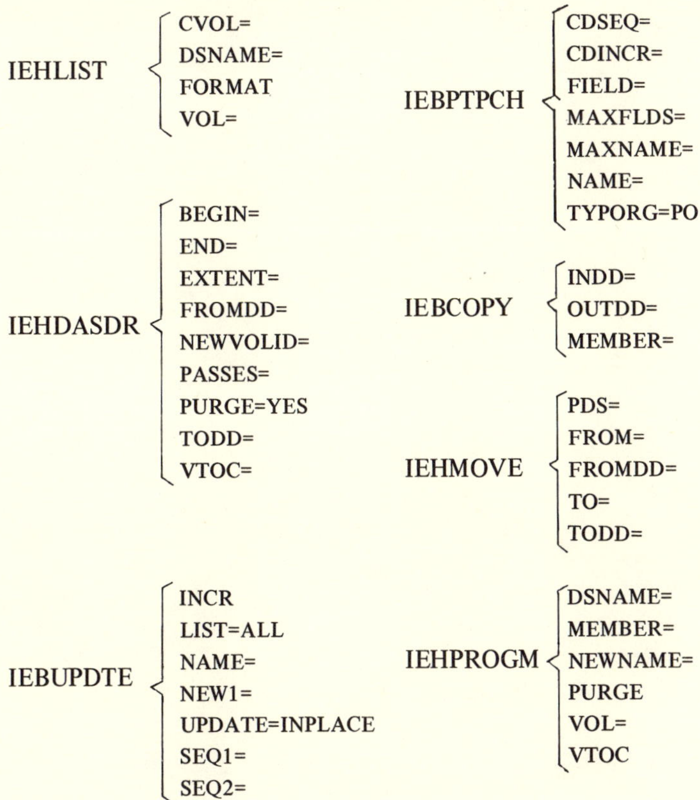

IEHLIST
- CVOL=
- DSNAME=
- FORMAT
- VOL=

IEBPTPCH
- CDSEQ=
- CDINCR=
- FIELD=
- MAXFLDS=
- MAXNAME=
- NAME=
- TYPORG=PO

IEHDASDR
- BEGIN=
- END=
- EXTENT=
- FROMDD=
- NEWVOLID=
- PASSES=
- PURGE=YES
- TODD=
- VTOC=

IEBCOPY
- INDD=
- OUTDD=
- MEMBER=

IEHMOVE
- PDS=
- FROM=
- FROMDD=
- TO=
- TODD=

IEBUPDTE
- INCR
- LIST=ALL
- NAME=
- NEW1=
- UPDATE=INPLACE
- SEQ1=
- SEQ2=

IEHPROGM
- DSNAME=
- MEMBER=
- NEWNAME=
- PURGE
- VOL=
- VTOC

The third list breaks it down even further, enumerating the parameters that
go with each of the action words. In other words, the action word describes

what action the Utility should do, and usually only two or three of these parameters are needed to further describe how and to what the action is to be done.

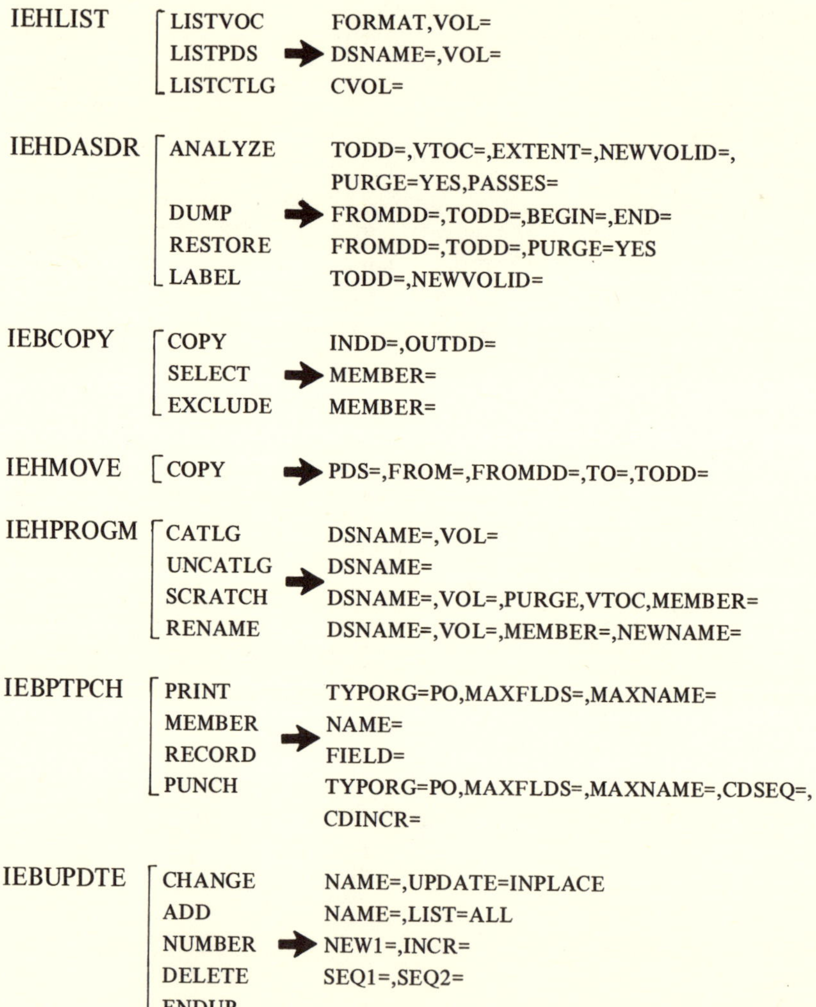

THE PARAMETERS

And last, the words can be divided according to what they are used to describe. Some give the name of a file, others specify numbers, and so on. Again, don't try to remember them, but try to get a feel for the ways they can be used.

1. Five are used to specify the name of a file or member that you may be listing, cataloging, changing, etc. These are:

    DSNAME= NAME= MEMBER= NEWNAME= PDS=

For example,

    DSNAME=SYS1.LINKLIB.

2. Five of these words can give the volume serial number of a pack or tape you are working on:

    NEWVOLID= VOL= CVOL= FROM= TO=

The VOL parameter on control cards, unlike the JCL, specifies the *unit type* as well as the disk or tape volume serial number, and they're connected by = signs. So to specify a disk pack D10040, just say:

    VOL=3330-D10040

For a tape 004000, just say:

    VOL=3400-3=004000

3. Fourteen of the words are used to specify numbers:

MAXFLDS=	END=	BEGIN=
INCR=	PASSES=	CDSEQ=
VTOC=	NEW1=	SEQ1=
FIELD=	CDINCR=	SEQ2=
EXTENT=	MAXNAME=	

For example, MAXFLDS=3 tells one Utility that the maximum number of fields is three (we'll come to what that means later).

4. Four words specify DDnames, to refer back to a file's DD card in the JCL. The DDname, as you remember, is the name of the DD card and begins in its third column, right after //. The four are:

    INDD= FROMDD= OUTDD= TODD=

For example, INDD=DISKFILE refers to the DD card with the name DISKFILE.

5. Four of the words are used to express a statement. They don't name anything; they state a fact or a desire. The word after the equal sign is always the same. You don't have to learn them now, but here they are, with their translations:

    TYPORG=PO "This type of file has a partitioned organization."
    PURGE=YES "Yes, purge (delete) all the files."
    UPDATE=INPLACE "Update the file in the space it already has."
    LIST=ALL "List all of it."

6. All of the terms so far have been followed by equal signs. Not so for the

final three words, which stand alone as statements. Here they are with their translations:

FORMAT   "I want it formatted."
PURGE   "I want it deleted."
VTOC   "I am referring to the whole VTOC."

Now, at least, these terms won't be completely new to you when you see them in the next section, which will go through each of the Utilities and describe how to have them perform each of their various functions.

As we go along we will accumulate a set of rules that sums up what DD cards and control cards are required for each function of each Utility.

CONTINUATION OF CONTROL CARDS

Before we start, note the rules for continuing the parameters of a control card onto a second card if they don't all fit on the first card.

1. The last complete parameter on the first card cannot go beyond column 70.
2. It must be followed by a comma indicating that you mean to continue onto a second card.
3. Put a nonblank character, such as an X or a C in column 72, to say that the card is to be continued.
4. On the second card, the parameters must continue, starting in column 16.

QUESTIONS

1. In the skeleton of JCL required for every Utility, give the first three cards that are always required.
2. What is the only thing that varies on these three cards?
3. If we wanted to use the Utility IEHLIST, what would the EXEC card look like?
4. *a.* What does the SYSPRINT DD card always have as its parameter?
   b. To what input/output device does this parameter refer?
   c. Why do you suppose all the Utilities require a SYSPRINT DD card? (What do they use it for?)
5. Besides the name of the Utility you want to use, what are the two other major variations in the cards you need to punch up to get your Utility to do what you want?
6. What does a Utility read to find out what you want it to do?
7. After what DD card does the control card go?

8. Does the control card begin with a // in columns 1 and 2, as do JCL cards?

9. *a.* On a control card, what is the main word called that the Utility looks at to see what it's supposed to do?

   b. Can it begin in column 1?

10. What follows the action word (after a blank, of course) to further describe what you want the Utility to do?

11. How many parameter words that go on control cards are described in this book?

12. Which Utility has no action words?

13. How does the VOL parameter on control cards differ from the VOL parameter on DD cards?

14. Can the DSNAME parameter on control cards be abbreviated as on DD cards?

15. *a.* If you want to continue a control card, what can't be in column 72 of the card that you wish to continue onto another card?

    b. Is this also true for continuing JCL cards?

16. *a.* In what column must the first parameter on the continuation card begin?

    b. Is this also true for continuing JCL cards?

4 IEHLIST

We begin with IEHLIST because it is the easiest Utility to use. The DD cards and control cards required to list the volume table of contents (VTOC), directory, or the catalog are simple and straightforward. Here we will begin accumulating our rules, which will summarize how to use the eight Utilities.

THE DD CARD

Since IEHLIST prints things each time from a specific disk pack, the DD card tells you *which* disk pack that is. And since, as in the case of the VTOC, you're not dealing with any particular file on the pack, you use the type of DD card that specifies the whole pack. (Refer back to the eighth type of DD card, on page 23.) And you can use any DDNAME to name the DD card.

If you want to list the VTOC or the directory of a file on pack D10040, the DD card could look like this:

```
//DISK  DD  UNIT=3330,VOL=SER=D10040,DISP=OLD
```

The same is true for the catalog. Just specify the disk pack or drum it is on. If it is on drum DD2305, the DD card would say:

```
//DRUM  DD  UNIT=2305,VOL=SER=DD2305,DISP=OLD
```

So now we have our first rule:

Rule 1. IEHLIST needs one DD card, for the disk pack you want information from, specifying the whole pack, with any DD name.

Now for the control cards required by IEHLIST.

The Control Cards

There are three different kinds of control cards, depending on what you want to have listed. They are simple and straightforward.

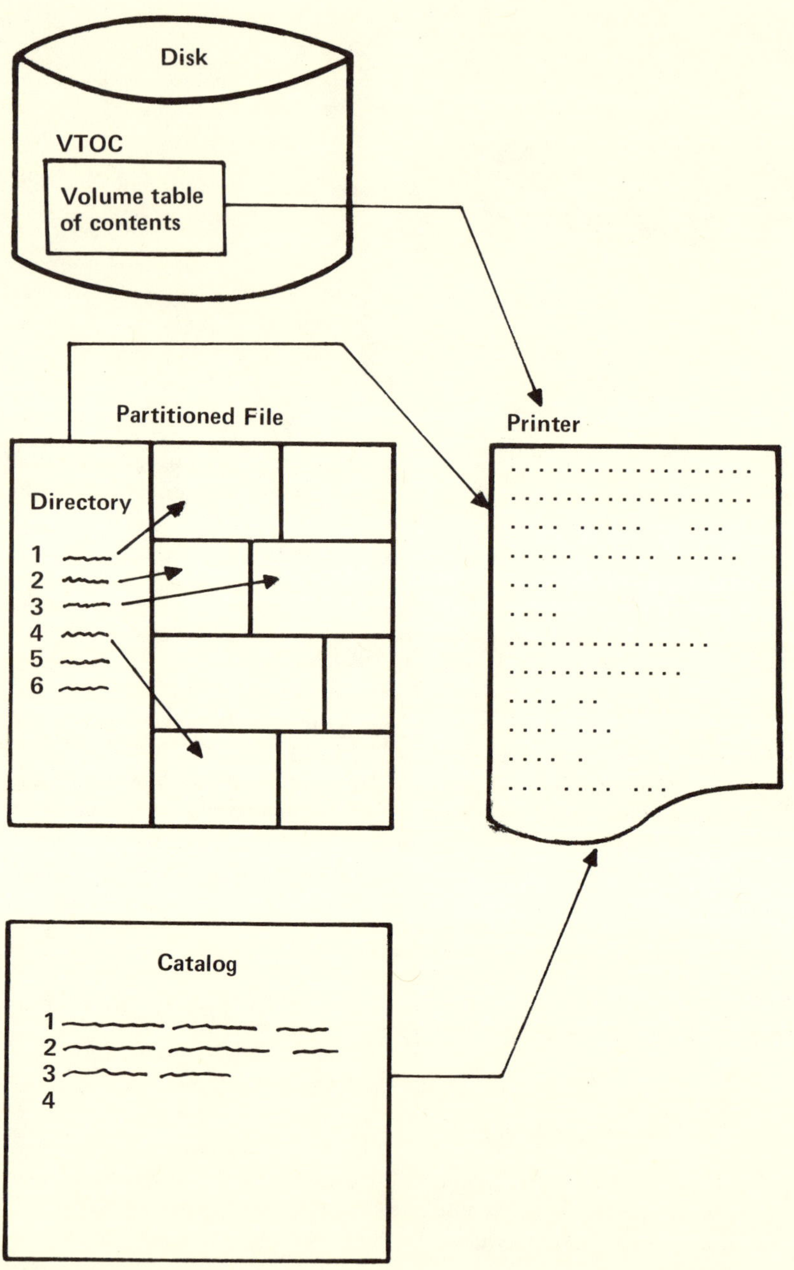

Fig. 4.1. IEHLIST prints out on the printer the volume table of contents (VTOC) of a disk, the directory of a partitioned file, or the catalog.

LISTVOC. The first one is used for listing a disk pack's volume table of contents. The action word needed is LISTVTOC, and the additional parameters are FORMAT and VOL. FORMAT means that you want the VTOC to be printed out in a readable format, and VOL tells which pack's VTOC you want listed. So, for pack D10040, the control card would be:

```
LISTVTOC  FORMAT,VOL=3330=D10040
```

This can be summed up simply as:

Rule 2. Printing a VTOC using IEHLIST requires one control card, and LISTVTOC is the action word. The parameters are: FORMAT, which stands alone; and VOL, which gives the unit type and the number of the pack whose VTOC is being listed.

The whole job would look like this:

```
//LISTVTOC       JOB       (accnt),NAME,MSGLEVEL=(1,1)
//STEP1          EXEC      PGM=IEHLIST
//SYSPRINT       DD        SYSOUT=A
//DISK           DD        UNIT=3330,VOL=SER=D10040,DISP=OLD
//SYSIN          DD        *
     LISTVTOC          FORMAT,VOL=3330=D10040
/*
//
```

LISTPDS. The second type of control card is used to list the directory of a partitioned file. A directory, you may remember, contains the names (in alphabetical order) of all the members of a partitioned file. Listing out this directory requires one control card for IEHLIST. The action word is LISTPDS (PDS stands for partitioned data set, which is another way of saying partitioned file). There are two parameters: DSNAME, which gives the name of the partitioned file; and VOL, which specifies the unit and volume serial number of the pack it is on. For example, say you wanted to find out what are the members in a file called LOADLIB, which happened to be on pack D10040. To list its directory, just say:

```
LISTPDS   DSNAME=LOADLIB,VOL=3330=D10040
```

Rule 3. Listing the directory of a partitioned file using IEHLIST requires one control card, and LISTPDS is the action word. The parameters are: DSNAME, to name the file; and VOL, to give the unit type and pack number the file is on.

Again, the whole job would look like this:

```
//LISTLIB        JOB       (accnt),NAME,MSGLEVEL=(1,1)
//STEP1          EXEC      PGM=IEHLIST
//SYSPRINT       DD        SYSOUT=A
//DISK           DD        UNIT=3330,VOL=SER=D10040,DISP=OLD
//SYSIN          DD        *
```

```
        LISTPDS    DSNAME-LOADLIB,VOL=3330=D10040
/*
//
```

LISTCTLG. The third type of control card lists the catalog. There is one primary catalog, which is always on the system pack or drum, and it contains the names of important files and the numbers of the disks or tapes that they are on. Listing out the catalog requires a very simple control card. All that goes on it is the action word LISTCTLG—that is all:

```
LISTCTLG
```

Rule 4. Listing the catalog using IEHLIST requires one control card, and
        LISTCTLG is the action word. There are no other parameters.
This would be the whole job, if the catalog is on drum DD2305:

```
//LISTCAT     JOB      (accnt),NAME,MSGLEVEL=(1,1)
//STEP1       EXEC     PGM=IEHLIST
//SYSPRINT    DD       SYSOUT=A
//DRUM        DD       UNIT=2305,VOL=SER=DD2305,DISP=OLD
//SYSIN       DD       *
       LISTCTLG
/*
//
```

A computer installation is also given the facility to have what is known as a secondary catalog. In this case, the primary catalog, which still has to be on the system pack or drum, can point to other catalogs that just continue the catalog. This is sometimes done to divide an overly large catalog into smaller, logical groups. A disk pack or drum that contains such a secondary catalog is called a control volume. If we want to list such a secondary catalog, we have to add another parameter to the LISTCTLG control card—CVOL (*control volume*), telling the unit type and volume serial number of the pack the secondary catalog is on. For example:

```
CVOL=3330=D10040
```

The whole control card would be:

```
LISTCTLG   CVOL=3330=D10040
```

which means "List the secondary catalog on D10040."

Rule 5. Listing a secondary catalog using IEHLIST requires one control card,
        and LISTCTLG is the action word. The one parameter is CVOL, where
        you give the unit type and serial number of the disk pack or drum
        that the secondary catalog is on.

The DD card, of course, now must be for the pack that the secondary catalog is on. The whole job for listing the secondary catalog on disk pack D10040 is:

```
//SECCATLG   JOB     (accnt),NAME,MSGLEVEL=(1,1)
//STEP1      EXEC    PGM=IEHLIST
//SYSPRINT   DD      SYSOUT=A
//DISK       DD      UNIT=3330,VOL=SER=D10040,DISP=OLD
//SYSIN      DD      *
        LISTCTLG   CVOL=3330=D10040
/*
//
```

QUESTIONS

1. Answer the following for the DD card required by IEHLIST.
    a. Is the DSNAME parameter required?
    b. What three parameters are required?
    c. What DD name can you use?
2. What action word on the control card do you use to do the following:
    a. List the volume table of contents.
    b. List the directory of a partitioned file.
    c. List the catalog.
3. What parameter is needed on the control cards for both listing the volume table of contents and listing the directory of a partitioned file?
4. Give the control card that would accomplish the following:
    a. List the VTOC of disk D10030.
    b. List the directory of a file named PARTFILE on disk D10040.
    c. List the main catalog.
    d. List the secondary catalog on disk D10030.
5. What do the letters CVOL stand for?
6. Give the DD cards that are necessary in the following instances:
    a. Listing the VTOC of disk D10020.
    b. Listing the directory of a file named LIBRARY on disk D10020.
    c. Listing the main catalog that is on disk D10040.
    d. Listing the secondary catalog on D10020.

5 IEHDASDR

IEHDASDR can initialize, relabel, dump, and restore disk packs. We'll deal
with each of these four functions separately.

INITIALIZING A NEW DISK PACK

This means putting on a volume serial number, reserving space for a volume
table of contents, and analyzing each track to see whether or not it can be
written on.

The DD Card

A new disk pack can only be mounted on a disk drive that is offline. If you
put it on one that is online, the system would tell you to remove it, saying "I
can't identify this disk because it has no volume serial number." So before
this job is run, put the new disk on an offline disk drive.

Now, filling out the DD card for such a disk presents some problems. First,
there is no way of describing with a DD card a disk that is offline; in addition,
the VOL=SER parameter can't be filled in for a disk that does not yet have a
volume serial number. This problem is overcome by leaving the DD card out,
and then referring in the control card to the offline drive that holds the disk.
We'll see how this is done when we come to the control card, but just remember that *there cannot be a DD card* because the disk has not yet been initialized.

The Control Card

ANALYZE is the action word, which means the same as INITIALIZE. There
are four parameters, which tell where the disk is, describe the VTOC, and assign a volume serial number. They are:

1. Initialize

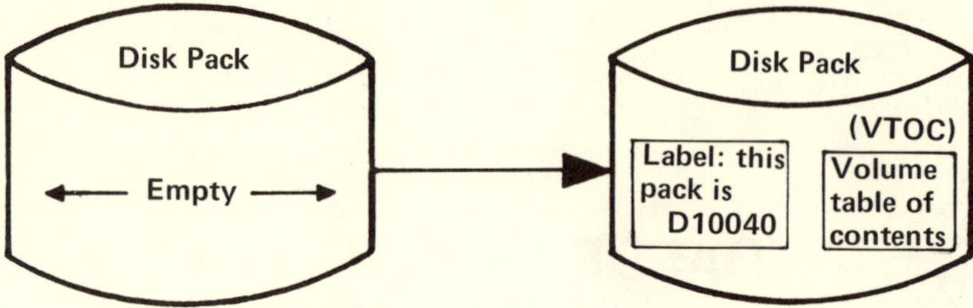

2. Relabel

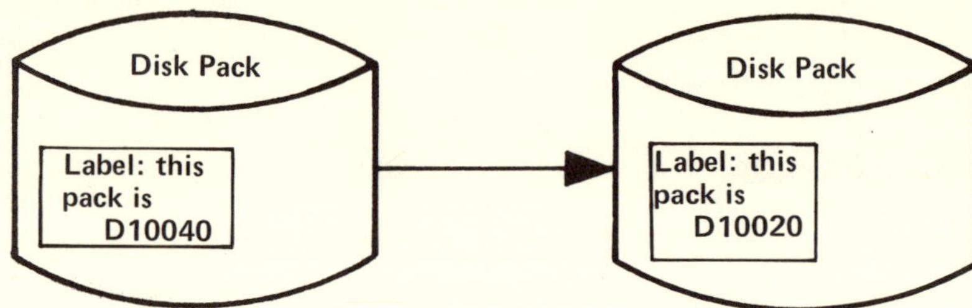

3. Dump—Restore

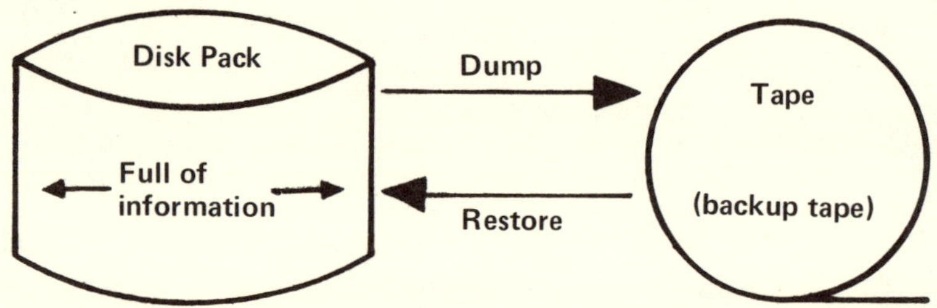

4. Print Tracks

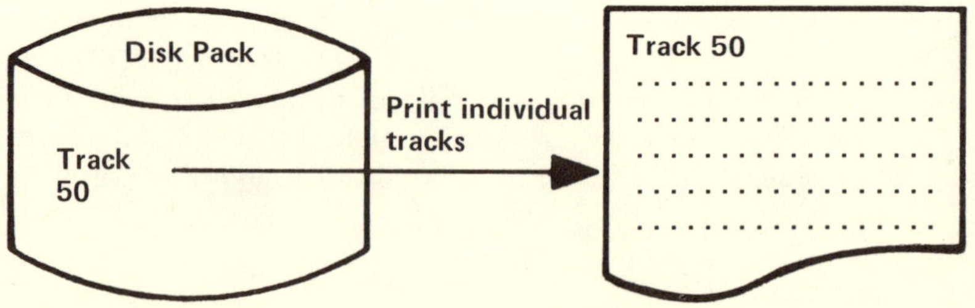

Fig. 5.1.   IEHDASDR can initialize, relabel, dump, and restore disk packs, and can print tracks.

TODD. Here you put the address of the offline disk drive where the new
disk pack was put. You would think that TODD (pronounced *too-dee-dee*)
would refer to the DD card for the disk that the Utility is going *to.* But
there is no DD card, and the only way to refer to an offline disk with no
volume serial number is by the actual drive it is on.
VTOC. This parameter tells on what track the VTOC is to begin. Usually,
the VTOC is put close in the middle of the pack, but for simplicity our
examples will show it as the beginning of the pack, but not at track Ø,
because that's where the volume serial number goes. So VTOC=1 puts it at
track 1.
EXTENT. This tells how many tracks long you want the VTOC to be. The
VTOC fits about 50 file description entries per track, so five to ten tracks
is usually enough. Thus, EXTENT=5.
NEWVOLID. Here you would give the six-character volume serial number
that you want the new disk pack to have. It can contain letters and numbers; NEWVOLID= D10040 assigns the volume serial number of D10040.
A sample control card would look like this:

    ANALYZE   TODD=230,VTOC=1,EXTENT=5,NEWVOLID=D10040

Rule 6. Initializing a new disk pack using IEHDASDR, requires no DD card,
       the disk must be offline. ANALYZE is the action word. The parameters
       are: TODD, to specify the offline disk drive; VTOC, which tells where
       the VTOC is to begin; EXTENT, which gives the length of the VTOC;
       and NEWVOLID, which assigns a volume serial number.
The whole job:

```
//INITLIZE        JOB     (accnt),NAME,MSGLEVEL=(1,1)
//STEP1           EXEC    PGM=IEHDASDR
//SYSPRINT        DD      SYSOUT=A
//SYSIN           DD      *
      ANALYZE        TODD=230,VTOC=1,EXTENT=5,NEWVOLID=D10040
/*
//
```

There is a fifth additional and optional parameter, which we won't include in
our example but will describe briefly because you may find it useful. It is:
PASSES. In addition to formatting the pack correctly, IEHDASDR also ex-
amines it for bad spots. This parameter tells how often you want it to
look at the whole pack for bad spots, because what it may not find out
on the first pass, it may find on subsequent passes. PASSES=3 means
"Check the pack three times for bad spots." You include this parameter
in the control card, and it would look like this:

ANALYZE   TODD=230,VTOC=1,EXTENT=5,NEWVOLID=D10040,PASSES=3

INITIALIZING AN OLD DISK PACK

Bad spots on a disk pack can cause input/output errors. When a pack is initialized, IEHDASDR, in addition to writing a volume serial number and VTOC, also checks to see if there are any bad spots. It does this by writing information on each track and then reading it back again, checking for errors. It then tells you if there are any errors and where (thus, the term *analyze*). Sometimes a pack that is already in use develops bad spots, and you might want to reinitialize it to have IEHDASDR see if and where they exist. You could use IEHDASDR as we did for the new pack, by varying it offline and using the JCL and control cards. But since an old pack already has a volume serial number, you don't need to vary it offline; you can leave the pack online. An *online* initialization is slightly different from the offline initialization just discussed. It can be done only with an old pack, one that already has a volume serial number. This reinitialization process writes over the information already on the pack, so before you run it, you may want to dump (back up) the pack to tape and then restore the information after you finish (using the DUMP and RESTORE functions of IEHDASDR, which we'll discuss in a moment).

The DD Card

Since in this case the pack is online, you need a DD card to describe it. It involves the whole pack and not any particular file on it, so use the type of DD card that describes the whole pack. Any DDname will do. If you are reinitializing pack D10040, the DD card would be:

```
//DISK   DD   UNIT=3330,VOL=SER=D10040,DISP=OLD
```

The Control Card

The control card for the *on*line reinitialization has two differences from the control card for the offline initialization. ANALYZE is still the action word, and the parameters VTOC, EXTENT, and NEWVOLID are used in exactly the same way. These are the two differences:

TODD. Here you don't put in the unit that the pack is on, but give the name of the DD card that describes the disk you want to reinitialize. This is because you now have a DD card for it, since it's online.

PURGE=YES. This says that it can write over any information on the pack while searching for I/O errors. This wasn't needed with the new pack because new packs are empty. This is how the control card looks:

```
ANALYZE   TODD=DISK,VTOC=1,EXTENT=5,NEWVOLID=D10040,     C
          PURGE=YES
```

Rule 7. Reinitializing a disk pack using IEHDASDR, the disk is left online, and one DD card, with any DDname, is needed for the whole pack. ANALYZE is the action word. The parameters VTOC, EXTENT, and NEWVOLID are the same as for the offline initialization, TODD names the DD card, and PURGE=YES allows it to erase information on the pack.

And the whole job for the online reinitialization is:

```
//ANALYZE        JOB     (accnt),NAME,MSGLEVEL=(1,1)
//STEP1          EXEC    PGM=IEHDASDR
//SYSPRINT       DD      SYSOUT=A
//DISK           DD      UNIT=3330,VOL=SER=D10040,DISP=OLD
//SYSIN          DD      *
     ANALYZE     TODD=DISK,VTOC=1,EXTENT=5,NEWVOLID=D10040,
                 PURGE=YES
/*
//
```

Incidentally, the PASSES parameter, described for the offline ANALYZE, can also be put on this control card to tell IEHDASDR to check the pack for bad spots more than once.

RELABELING A DISK PACK

One of the minor functions of initializing an old pack is that you can assign a pack a new volume serial number. IEHDASDR also gives you the facility to give any pack a new volume serial number without initializing the pack, too. This way you don't destroy the information on it. This is called relabeling the disk pack.

The DD Card

The DD card is the same as for initializing an old pack—it just refers to the pack you are relabeling. The volume serial number in the DD card refers to the *old* volume serial number, because that is the number the system needs in order to get the pack mounted before your job can start. The DD card:

```
//DISK   DD   UNIT=3330,VOL=SER=D10040,DISP=OLD
```


The Control Card

The action word is LABEL. There are two parameters, taken right from the ANALYZE control card, and their meanings are the same.

TODD. Refers to the name of the DD card that describes the disk you are relabeling.

NEWVOLID. This is, again, the new volume serial number you are having put on the pack.

The control card to change the volume serial number to D10041 is:

```
LABEL   TODD=DISK,NEWVOLID=D10041
```

Rule 8. Giving an old pack a new volume serial number by using IEHDASDR is called relabeling a disk pack. It has one DD card, referring to the whole pack being relabeled. The action word on the control card is LABEL, and the two parameters are: TODD, naming the DD card; and NEWVOLID, giving the new volume serial number.

The whole job:

```
//RELABEL     JOB     (accnt),NAME,MSGLEVEL=(1,1)
//STEP1       EXEC    PGM=IEHDSDR
//SYSPRINT    DD      SYSOUT=A
//DISK        DD      UNIT=3330,VOL=SER=D10040,DISP=OLD
//SYSIN       DD      *
     LABEL       TODD=DISK,NEWVOLID=D10041
/*
//
```

CREATING A BACKUP TAPE

This involves taking all the information on a disk and dumping it to tape to save it just in case something goes wrong on the disk.

The DD Cards

Here we're working with two files, the disk *from* which we're dumping information, and a new tape *to* which we're dumping the information, so we need two DD cards. The one for the disk should again refer to the whole disk and can have any DDname. Simply, for disk D10040 it would be:

```
//DISK   DD   UNIT=3330,VOL=SER=D10040,DISP=OLD
```

The tape is a new tape we're creating, so refer to the sixth type of file, described way back. This type of DD card needs three parameters: DSNAME, with any name you choose; UNIT=3400-3; and DISP=(NEW,KEEP). Use any DDname. So it looks like this:

```
//TAPE   DD   DSN=TAPE,UNIT=3400-3,DISP=(NEW,KEEP)
```

The Control Card

The action word, predictably, is DUMP. And we have two parameters:
FROMDD. Here you specify the name that you gave to the DD card for
the *disk*, since that's what you're dumping *from.*
TODD. Here you specify the name that you gave to the DD card for the
tape, since that's what you're dumping *to.*
Assuming that you've named those two DD cards DISK and TAPE, the whole
control card looks like this:

    DUMP   FROMDD=DISK,TODD=TAPE

Rule 9. Creating a backup tape using IEHDASDR requires two DD cards, one
   for the disk you're dumping from (specifying the whole pack), and
   the other for the tape you're dumping to (specifying a new tape). On
   the control card, DUMP is the action word. The parameters are:
   FROMDD, giving the name of the disk DD card; and TODD, giving the
   name of the tape DD card.

The whole job:

```
//DUMP       JOB     (accnt),NAME,MSGLEVEL=(1,1)
//STEP1      EXEC    PGM=IEHDASDR
//SYSPRINT   DD      SYSOUT=A
//DISK       DD      UNIT=3330,VOL=SER=D10040,DISP=OLD
//TAPE       DD      DSN=TAPE,UNIT=3400-3,DISP=(NEW,KEEP)
//SYSIN      DD      *
       DUMP   FROMDD=DISK,TODD=TAPE
/*
//
```

PRINTING SPECIFIC TRACKS

Dumping a disk pack usually means dumping it to a tape. But you can also
dump it to a printer. Now this means that you can look at the actual letters
and numbers out on the disk pack. Whatever is on the pack gets dumped to
the printer, just as it is, for you to look at.

The DD Cards and the Control Card

This is very similar to dumping a disk pack to tape, but there are two differences. First, we don't need a DD card for the tape file. We're going to dump
the disk to the SYSPRINT file. The other change is that two new parameters
are added to the control card, specifying what tracks are to be printed:

BEGIN. Here you give eight numbers, the first four being the number of
the first cylinder you want printed, the next four being the first track on
that cylinder you want printed. In other words, BEGIN=00050002 means
start printing with cylinder 5 track 2. There must be eight numbers.
END. In this case, there must be eight numbers in the same format, giving
the last cylinder and track you want printed.

For example,

    BEGIN=00050002,END=00060002

means print from cylinder 5 track 2 to cylinder 6 track 2—21 tracks in all.
The whole control card would be:

    DUMP   FROMDD=DISK,TODD=SYSPRINT,BEGIN=00050002,END=00060002.

Notice that we say TODD=SYSPRINT to indicate that we are dumping to the
printer, to the SYSPRINT file, which will also have any messages sent to us by
IEHDASDR.

Incidentally, if you want to print just one track, BEGIN and END refer to
the same track. For example, to print just cylinder 5 track 2, say:

    BEGIN=00050002,END=00050002

Rule 10. Printing specific tracks of a disk pack using IEHDASDR is part of
the dump function, and is the same as dumping the pack to tape except that the DD card for the tape is left out. The TODD parameter
refers to the SYSPRINT file (dumping to the printer), and the two
new parameters are BEGIN and END, giving the cylinder and track
numbers (eight hexadecimal numbers in all) with which to start and
stop printing.

The whole job:

```
//PRINTRKS      JOB     (accnt),NAME,MSGLEVEL=(1,1)
//STEP1         EXEC    PGM=IEHDASDR
//SYSPRINT      DD      SYSOUT=A
//DISK          DD      UNIT=3330,VOL=SER=D10040,DISP=OLD
//SYSIN         DD      *
          DUMP       FROMDD=DISK,TODD=SYSPRINT,BEGIN=0005002,       C
               END=00060002
/*
//
```

There's a trick here that must be explained before we go on. The numbering
system that we normally count with has ten numbers in it, 0 through 9, and it
is called the decimal numbering system. When we count and get to the number 9, we start a new column and continue counting from there—10, 11, 12,

etc. The computer uses a different numbering system to count the cylinders and tracks of a disk; it is called the hexadecimal numbering system and has 16 numbers, not 10. Here they are:

0, 1, 2, 3, 4, 5, 6, 7, 8, 9, A, B, C, D, E, F

As you can see, when we get past the normal number 9, we don't start a new column, but continue in the same column with letters A through F. The letters have the following equivalent in decimal:

hexadecimal	*decimal*
A	10
B	11
C	12
D	13
E	14
F	15

To count above F in hexadecimal does require a new column, and the number after F is 10. So to continue the chart:

hexadecimal	*decimal*
E	14
F	15
10	16
11	17
12	18

In other words, the same written number has a different value in hexadecimal or decimal. The hexadecimal number 20, for example, equals the decimal number 32.

Unfortunately, IEHDASDR requires that you specify the cylinder and track addresses in hexadecimal. To convert the decimal cylinder or track address to hexadecimal, follow this procedure:

1. Divide the decimal number by 16, and get a result and a remainder.
2. If either the result or the remainder is from 10 to 15, convert it to the letters A through F using the chart above.
3. Make the result the first digit of your answer, and make the remainder the second digit of your answer.

Example 1. Convert the decimal number 100 to hexadecimal.

$$
\begin{array}{r}
6 \\
16\,\overline{)100} \\
\underline{96} \\
4
\end{array}
$$

result: = 6
remainder: = 4
answer: = 64

Example 2. Convert the decimal number 110 to hexadecimal.

$$\begin{array}{r} 6 \\ 16\,\overline{)110} \\ \underline{96} \\ 14 \end{array}$$

result: = 6
remainder: = 14 = E
answer: = 6E

So to print from cylinder 100 track 1 to cylinder 110 track 10, say:

    BEGIN=00640001,END=006E000A

With practice, you will be able to get it easily. (Anything new seems complicated at first.)

RESTORING A DISK FROM A BACKUP TAPE

If you're lucky enough to have a backup tape for a pack that develops problems, you'll want to restore the pack by moving the information from the tape back onto the disk.

The DD Cards

This is the exact reverse of creating the backup tape because now you're going *from tape to disk.* So again we have two DD cards, one for the tape and one for the disk. The DD card for the tape is different from the one we used when we created the tape, because now it is OLD. Refer back to the DD card for an old, uncataloged tape—which is file type number 3 (described in the JCL section). As you see, four parameters are required. DSNAME must specify the name you gave the tape when you created it (in this case, its name is TAPE). Then comes UNIT=3400-3, identifying it as a tape. The VOL=SER parameter must give the volume serial number of the backup tape. Last comes DISP=OLD. Any DD name will do. If the tape number is 004000, the DD card for the backup tape looks like this:

    //TAPE   DD   DSNAME=TAPE,UNIT=3400-3,VOL=SER=004000,DISP=OLD

The DD card for the disk, however, is the same as before, because we're still referring to the whole pack, and that is file type number 8. It looks like this:

```
//DISK   DD   UNIT=3330,VOL=SER=D10040,DISP=OLD
```

So in restoring a disk from a backup tape, the only difference in the DD cards from when we were creating the backup tape is the one for the tape, because the tape is OLD, when then it was NEW.

Note: At the beginning of most tapes is a label that contains, among other things, the DSNAME of the file on the tape. You have to specify this DSNAME on the DD card when you want to use the tape. If you give the wrong name, the system gives you an 813 completion code. There is a trick you can use if you don't know the right DSNAME. Just have this name check bypassed by saying on the DD card LABEL=(2,BLP) (BLP stands for bypass label processing). The rest of the DD card is the same, so it then looks like this:

```
//TAPE   DD   DSNAME=TAPE,UNIT=3400-3,VOL=SER=004000,LABEL=(2,BLP),
//             DISP=OLD
```

Use this technique only when you have to.

The Control Card

The action word, as you might guess, is RESTORE. There are three parameters, all of which are familiar:

FROMDD. Now we're going *from* the tape *to* the disk. So here, put the name you gave to the DD card describing the tape. In this case, it's FROMDD=TAPE.

TODD. And likewise, here put the name you gave to the DD card describing the disk, because that's where you're going *to.* Here it's TODD=DISK.

PURGE=YES. This means the same as it did before: "If you find any information still on the disk, you can write over it with the information from the backup tape."

The whole control card would read:

```
RESTORE   FROMDD=TAPE,TODD=DISK,PURGE=YES
```

Rule 11. Restoring a disk from a backup tape using IEHDASDR requires two DD cards; one is for the tape you are restoring from, specifying an OLD tape (DSNAME,VOL=SER=,UNIT=,DISP=OLD); the other is for the disk you are restoring to, specifying the whole disk. On the control card, RESTORE is the action word. The parameters are: FROMDD, naming the DD card for the tape; TODD, naming the DD card for the disk; and PURGE=YES, allowing it to erase any information still on the disk.

The whole job would then look like this:

```
//RESTORE   JOB     (accnt),NAME,MSGLEVEL=(1,1)
```

```
//STEP1         EXEC    PGM=IEHDASDR
//SYSPRINT      DD      SYSOUT=A
//TAPE          DD      DSN=TAPE,VOL=SER=004000,UNIT=3400-3,DISP=OLD
//DISK          DD      UNIT=3330,VOL=SER=D10040,DISP=OLD
//SYSIN         DD      *
    RESTORE     FROMDD=TAPE,TODD=DISK,PURGE=YES
/*
//
```

QUESTIONS

1. What kind of disk drive does a disk pack that is to be initialized for the first time have to be put on?

2. What kind of DD card is necessary for initializing a disk pack for the first time?

3. What two things are put on the disk pack when initializing it?

4. What action word tells IEHDASDR to initialize a disk pack?

5. If there is no DD card for a first-time initialization, what does the TODD parameter refer to?

6. Give the VTOC and EXTENT parameters that would have the VTOC start at track 1 and be ten tracks long.

7. What parameter is used to specify the volume serial number the disk is to have?

8. How would you get IEHDASDR to check the disk four times for bad spots, instead of the normal once-over?

9. Why would someone reinitialize a disk pack that already has a volume serial number and a VTOC?

10. Does such a disk pack have to be on an offline disk drive?

11. Can you have a DD card for such a disk pack?

12. What does the TODD parameter in the reinitialization refer to?

13. What is the action word on the control card for the reinitialization of a disk pack?

14. What is the only parameter that goes on the control card for a reinitialization as opposed to a first-time initialization, and what does it mean?

15. *a.* What action word would you use to give the disk pack a new volume serial number?

    b. What two parameters are needed?

16. Let's say we're changing the volume serial number of disk D10020 to D10025:

    a. Give the control card needed.

    b. Give the DD card needed.

17. What is the action word needed to do the following:
    a. Put the contents of a disk pack onto a backup tape.
    b. Print what's on specific tracks of a disk pack.
    c. Put the contents of a backup tape back onto a disk pack.
18. What are the two parameters needed on the control cards for either a DUMP or RESTORE operation?
19. When printing specific tracks of a disk pack, what file does the TODD parameter of the control card refer to?
20. Give the BEGIN and END parameters needed to print from cylinder 8 track 1 to cylinder 30 track 11.
21. What is the DISP parameter on the DD card for the tape file in the following instances:
    a. Creating a backup tape.
    b. Using a backup tape to restore the contents of a disk pack.
22. Assuming that the DD cards for the disk and tape files have the DDnames DISK and TAPE, respectively, give the control card for the following actions:
    a. Creating a backup tape.
    b. Using a backup tape to restore the contents of a disk pack.
23. Give the DD card for disk D10020 for the following processes:
    a. Dumping its contents to a tape.
    b. Restoring its contents from a tape.
    c. Printing tracks from it.
    d. Reinitializing it.
24. Give the DD card for tape 002000 in the following instances:
    a. Dumping the contents of a disk pack to it.
    b. Using it to restore the contents of a disk pack.
25. Give the whole control card to print cylinder 50 track 5 of a disk pack.
26. Convert the number 200 to hexadecimal.

6 IEBGENER

IEBGENER is a very easy and handy utility to use. It is basically used to convert a normal sequential file from one input/output device to another. Considering that the four input/output devices are the card reader/punch, tape, disk, and the printer, these are the possibilities:

    cards to tape, disk, printer, or cards
    tape to tape, disk, printer, or cards
    disk to tape, disk, printer, or cards

It is, in effect, a "duplicating" utility. Its most common functions are putting a card file on tape, copying one tape to another tape, and printing a tape.

The DD Cards

The DD name for the input file, as in many other Utilities, is SYSUT1. Since the input can be cards or an old file on disk or tape, just select the parameters needed to describe that type of file. If the input is on cards, the DD card would be—

    //SYSUT1 DD *

—followed by the cards themselves. If the input file is an old file on tape (file type 3) or an old file on disk (file type 2), it requires DSNAME, UNIT, VOL=SER, and DISP=OLD. For example, on tape:

    //SYSUT1   DD   DSN=TAPE,UNIT=3400-3,VOL=SER=004000,DISP=OLD

There's a nice little trick that can be mentioned here. Even though a partitioned file is not, by definition, a sequential file, each of its members individually is sequential. So IEBGENER can also be used to print or punch out a member of a partitioned file (usually a card image partitioned file). The way you do this is to put the member name you want printed or punched in parentheses after the DSname on the SYSUT1 (input) DD card. For example—

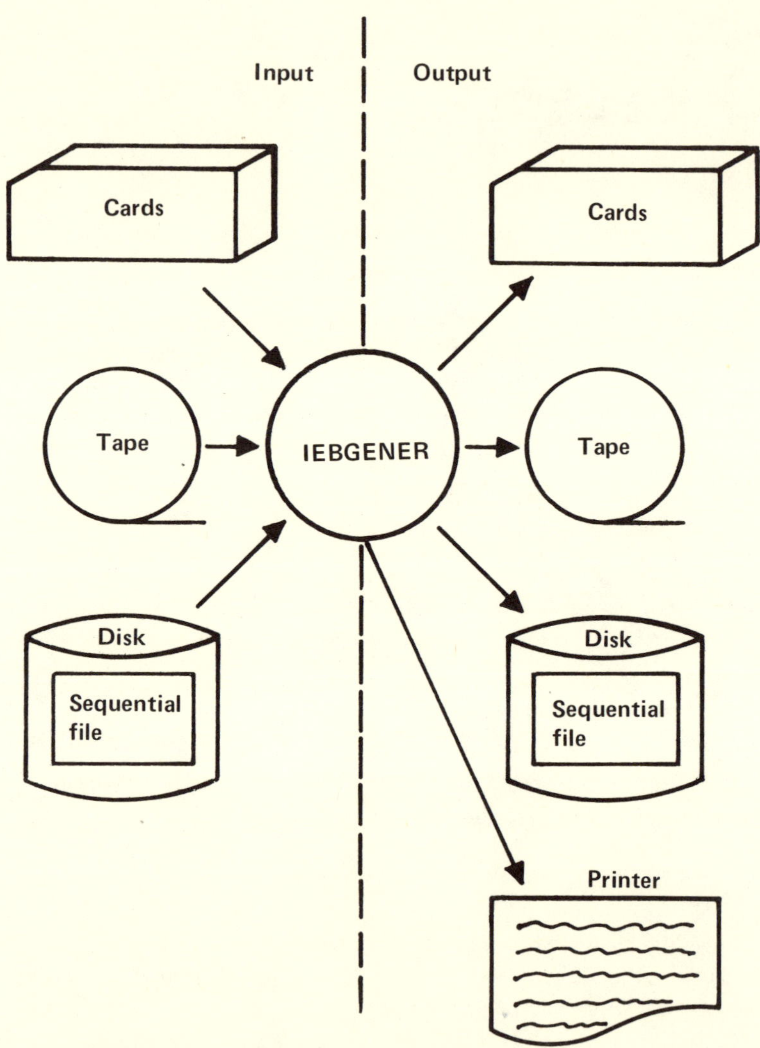

Fig. 6.1. IEBGENER can take a sequential file on cards, tape, or disk and duplicate it, creating a new sequential file on cards, tape, disk, or printer (printing it out).

```
    DSNAME=PARTFILE(MEMBER)
```

—would refer to the member called MEMBER in the partitioned file called
PARTFILE.
A whole DD card would be:

```
//SYSUT1   DD   DSNAME=PARTFILE(MEMBER),UNIT=3330,
//              VOL=SER=D10040,DISP=SHR
```

The DDname for the output file is SYSUT2. You can have this file be the
printer, a card punch, or a new file on disk or tape, depending on where you
want the input file copied to. But it's on this output file DD card that we
come across the one tricky thing about IEBGENER, and to describe it requires
defining a new term.

The amount of information that is read from a tape or disk at one time is
called a block of information. Now, when a card that has 80 columns of information is transferred to a tape or a disk, those 80 columns of information
are called a record. These records can be blocked together to form any even
multiple of 80—160, 240, 800, 1600, etc. This way, the blocks are larger and
more records can be read from the disk or tape file for every read. This can
save input/output time. The size you choose for the block is called the blocksize.

On a DD card, you can specify how big a blocksize you want with the
following parameter:

```
    DCB=BLKSIZE=
```

For example, if the blocksize you choose is 800, you say:

```
    DCB=BLKSIZE=800
```

For some reason, IEBGENER requires that you put this parameter on all
SYSUT2 DD cards, including those for the printer and the card punch. Re-
member it. IEBGENER won't work without it. Let's make it a separate rule.
Rule 12. IEBGENER requires a special parameter on its SYSUT2 (output) DD
         card—DCB=BLKSIZE= —where you specify how big you want to block
         the information on the output file. The blocksize must be an even
         multiple of the size of a record. For the card punch, it is always
         DCB=BLKSIZE=80 (unblocked); for the printer, it is always equal to
         the size of one record (also not blocked).
There are four possibilities for the SYSUT2 DD card. In the following example, we've chosen a blocksize of 80, but you must check the size of the
records on your input file before you choose, because the blocksize must be
an even multiple of the record size.

Printer:

    //SYSUT2 DD SYSOUT=A,DCB=BLKSIZE=80

Card punch:

    //SYSUT2 DD SYSOUT=B,DCB=BLKSIZE=80

New file on tape (file type 6):

    //SYSUT2 DD DSN=TAPE,UNIT=3400-3,DISP=(NEW,KEEP),DCB-BLKSIZE=80

New file on disk (file type 5):

    //SYSUT2 DD DSN=DISK,UNIT=3330,DISP=(NEW,KEEP),VOL=SER=D10040,
    //   SPACE=(CYL,10),DCB=BLKSIZE=80

We included the VOL=SER parameter for the disk file because you'd usually
have a specific disk you want the file copied to. In the same way, you can include the VOL=SER parameter for the tape file if you want to copy to a specific tape. The SPACE parameter for the disk file here is an arbitrary size—just
make it as large as you need.

The Control Card

The only complicated part of IEBGENER is the JCL for the DD cards.
There is no control card needed at all. IEBGENER knows what to do without
a control card—it just copies from the input file (SYSUT1) to the output file
(SYSUT2). So to indicate the absence of a control card, change the SYSIN DD
card to:

    //SYSIN   DD   DUMMY

Rule 13. IEBGENER copies information from an input file to an output file.
        The name of the DD card for the input file must be SYSUT1, and
        can be cards (//SYSIN DD *) or an old file on tape or disk (DSN,
        UNIT, VOL=SER, DISP). The name of the DD card for the output file
        must be SYSUT2, which can be the printer (SYSOUT=A), punched
        cards (SYSOUT=B), a new file on tape (DSN, UNIT, DISP), or a new
        file on disk (DSN, UNIT, VOL=SER, DISP, SPACE). The DCB=BLKSIZE
        parameter must also be on this card. No control card is needed, and
        its absence is indicated by a //SYSIN DD DUMMY card.
    We'll give three examples of its most common uses:
Copying tape to tape:

    //DUPTAPE   JOB   (accnt),NAME,MSGLEVEL=(1,1)
    //STEP1   EXEC   PGM=IEBGENER
    //SYSPRINT   DD   SYSOUT=A

```
//SYSUT1      DD      DSN=TAPE,UNIT=3400-3,VOL=SER=004000,DISP=OLD
//SYSUT2      DD      DSN=TAPE,UNIT=3400-3,DISP=(NEW,KEEP),
//                    DCB=BLKSIZE=80
//SYSIN       DD      DUMMY
```

Tape to print:

```
//PRNTTAPE  JOB    (accnt),NAME,MSGLEVEL=(1,1)
//STEP1     DD     PGM=IEBGENER
//SYSPRINT  DD     SYSOUT=A
//SYSUT1    DD     DSN=TAPE,UNIT=3400-3,VOL=SER=004000,DISP=OLD
//SYSUT2    DD     SYSOUT=A,DCB=BLKSIZE=80
//SYSIN     DD     DUMMY
```

Card to tape:

```
//CARDTAPE  JOB    (accnt),NAME,MSGLEVEL=(1,1)
//STEP1     EXEC   PGM=IEBGENER
//SYSPRINT  DD     SYSOUT=A
//SYSUT1    DD     *
```

> [*card file to be put on tape goes here*]

```
/*
//SYSUT2  DD   DSN=TAPE,UNIT=3400-3,DISP=(NEW,KEEP),DCB=BLKSIZE=80
//SYSIN     DD   DUMMY
```

QUESTIONS

1. Does IEBGENER work with sequential or partitioned files?
2. What is the DD name for these files:
   a. Input file.
   b. Output file.
3. Does IEBGENER need any control cards?
4. What does the SYSIN DD card always look like?
5. From what three types of devices can IEBGENER copy?
6. What four parameters are needed on the SYSUT1 DD card if the input file to be duplicated is on tape or disk (and is not cataloged)?
7. Give the SYSUT1 DD card required if the input is as follows:
   a. Cards.
   b. A file named SEQFILE on disk D10020 (not cataloged).
   c. A file named TAPEFILE on tape 002000 (not cataloged).
   d. A member called MEM1 of a file called LIBFILE on disk D10025 (not cataloged).
8. What unusual parameter must always go on the SYSUT2 DD card?

9. What is the relationship between the size of a record on a file and the size of a block on the same file?

10. For printers or card reader/punches, can the blocksize be any larger than the size of an individual record?

11. Are all the following on a file usually the same size?
    a. Records
    b. Blocks

12. What are the four types of devices to which IEBGENER can copy?

13. Assume that you have an input file with a record size of 80. Give the SYSUT2 DD cards if you want to do the following:
    a. Print the file.
    b. Punch the file.

14. What DISP parameter is needed for the SYSUT2 DD card if the output is to go on disk or tape?

15. Again assume an input record size of 80, but now we want an output blocksize of 800. Give the SYSUT2 DD card if we want to create an output file called FILE on the following:
    a. A tape (we don't care which tape).
    b. Disk D10020, giving it 40 cylinders of disk space.

7 IEBCOPY

IEBCOPY copies and compresses partitioned files, and only partitioned files.
Before we get to the specific things it can do, let's first discuss two special
DD cards it always needs.

THE TWO SPECIAL DD CARDS FOR IEBCOPY

As IEBCOPY does its copying, it always uses two temporary work files on
disk to hold temporary information. You have to include a DD card for each
of these two files. The name for the first card always must be SYSUT3, and the
name for the second card always must be SYSUT4. A temporary work file on
disk, which was described in the JCL section as file type number 7, needs only
two parameters: UNIT and SPACE. UNIT=3330 says that it's on disk. And since
IEBCOPY usually doesn't need more than five tracks of space for each temporary file, SPACE=(TRK,5) will specify that. DD cards for these two files always
look exactly like this:

```
//SYSUT3   DD   UNIT=3330,SPACE=(TRK,5)
//SYSUT4   DD   UNIT=3330,SPACE=(TRK,5)
```

They are needed every time you use IEBCOPY.

Rule 14. IEBCOPY always uses two temporary work files on disk, and a DD
card is needed for each (UNIT and SPACE parameters needed only.)
The DDnames must be SYSUT3 and SYSUT4; each usually needs
about five tracks of space.

COPYING FROM DISK TO DISK

IEBCOPY can copy a partitioned file from one disk to another. This copies
the whole partitioned file to another disk pack, perhaps because you need the
first disk pack for something else.

"

1. Copy a whole partitioned file to a new disk pack

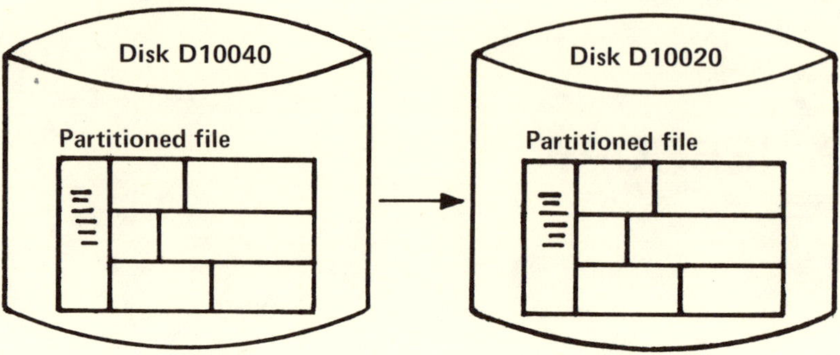

2. Copy single members from one partitioned file to another

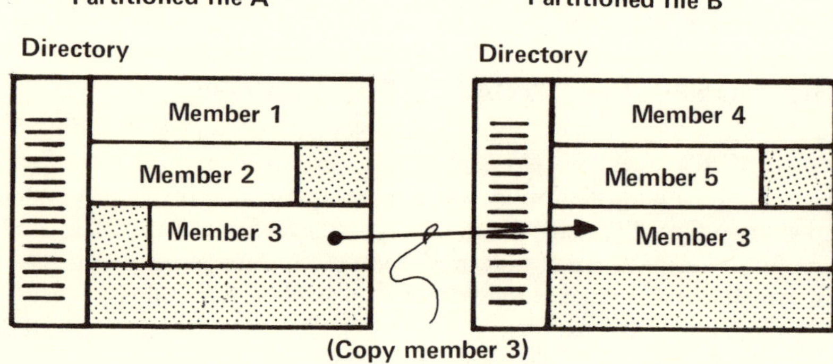

3. Compress a partitioned file

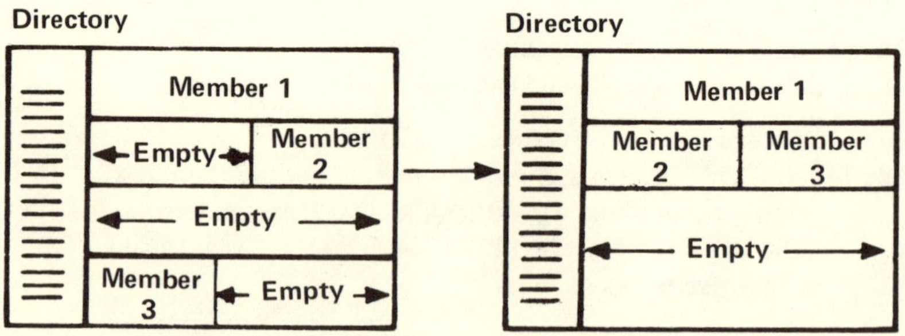

Fig. 7.1. IEBCOPY can copy or compress a partitioned file, or can copy an individual member from one partitioned file to another.

The DD Cards

This process involves two files, the OLD file from which you are copying
and the NEW file to which you are copying. So two DD cards are needed. They
can have any DDnames. The first file is an OLD file on disk. Refer back to file
type number 1 in the JCL section. The DD card for such a file needs four
parameters: DSNAME, UNIT, VOL=SER, and DISP=OLD. For example, if the
name of the file is FROMLIB and it is on disk D10040, the DD would look like
this:

```
//FROM   DD   DSNAME=FROMLIB,UNIT=3330,VOL=SER=D10040,DISP=OLD
```

As we said before, the card can have any DDname—in this case, we gave it
the name FROMLIB. The second DD card is slightly more complicated. This
second file is the NEW file on disk to which we are copying the first file, so
for this refer back to file type number 5 in the JCL section. The DD card for
the new file on disk has five parameters: DSNAME, UNIT, VOL=SER, DISP=
(NEW,KEEP), and SPACE. Let's say the name of this new file we are creating
is TOLIB, that we are putting it on disk D10080, and that we are reserving
400 tracks for it. This is the DD card:

```
//TO   DD   DSNAME=TOLIB,UNIT=3330,VOL=SER=D10080,DISP=(NEW,KEEP),
//               SPACE (TRK,(400,,50))
```

This DD card is difficult enough, but in addition we see something new in
the space parameter (the number 50) which hasn't been discussed yet. This reserves space for the directory of the partitioned file we are creating. The number should be equal to about one-third of the number of members that the
partitioned file will contain. So, if the file will hold 150 members, put down
the number 50. Let's take another look:

```
SPACE=(TRK,(400,,50))
```

Notice that there must be two commas between the number 400 and the
number 50. So, to copy a partitioned file from one disk to another requires,
if we include two temporary files, four DD cards in all. Here they are for our
example:

```
//FROM        DD   DSNAME=FROMLIB,UNIT=3330,VOL=SER=D10040,
//                 DISP=OLD
//TO          DD   DSNAME=TOLIB,UNIT=3330,VOL=SER=D10080,
//                 DISP=(NEW,KEEP),
             SPACE=(TRK,(400,,50))
//SYSUT3      DD   UNIT=3330,SPACE=(TRK,5)
//SYSUT4      DD   UNIT=3330,SPACE=(TRK,5)
```

The Control Card

The action word is COPY, and there are two parameters:
INDD=. Here you specify the name you gave to the DD card for the file
from which you are copying. It is the *input.* In our example, that card
was named FROM, so you'd write IND=FROM.
OUTDD=. As you might suspect, here you specify the name you gave to
the DD card for the file to which you are copying. It is the *output.* In our
example, that card was named TO, so you'd write OUTDD=TO.
The whole control card would look like this:

```
COPY   INDD=FROM,OUTDD=TO
```

Rule 15. Copying a partitioned file from one disk to another using IEBCOPY
requires four DD cards: two for the work files SYSUT3 and SYSUT4
plus one for the old file you are copying from (DSNAME, UNIT,
VOL=SER, DISP) and one for the new file you are copying to
(DSNAME, UNIT, VOL=SER, DISP, SPACE), both with any DDnames.
There is one control card, and COPY is the action word. The two
parameters are: INDD, giving the name of the DD card describing the
OLD file; and OUTDD, giving the name of the DD card describing the
NEW file.

The whole job would look like this:

```
//COPY          JOB     (accnt),NAME,MSGLEVEL=(1,1)
//STEP1         EXEC    PGM=IEBCOPY
//SYSPRINT      DD      SYSOUT=A
//FROM          DD      DSN=FROMLIB,UNIT=3330,VOL=SER=D10040,
//                      DISP=OLD
//TO            DD      DSN=TOLIB,UNIT=3330,VOL=SER=D10080,
//                      DISP=(NEW,KEEP),
               SPACE=(TRK,(400,,50))
//SYSUT3        DD      UNIT=3330,SPACE=(TRK,5)
//SYSUT4        DD      UNIT=3330,SPACE=(TRK,5)
//SYSIN         DD      *
       COPY     INDD=FROM,OUTDD=TO
/*
//
```

COPYING INDIVIDUAL MEMBERS FROM ONE
PARTITIONED FILE TO ANOTHER

In this case, we are working with two full-fledged OLD partitioned files and
simply transferring individual members from one to another.

The DD Cards

Besides the two DD cards for the work files SYSUT3 and SYSUT4, there are two other DD cards, one for the file from which you are copying the members and the other for the files to which you are copying. They are both OLD files on disk, so both the DD cards conform to the rule for file type number 1 (DSNAME, UNIT, VOL=SER, DISP). They can have any DD name. If the first file is called FROMLIB and is on disk D10040, the DD card is:

    //FROM DD DSNAME=FROMLIB,UNIT=3330,VOL=SER=D10040,DISP=OLD

Likewise, if the second file is called TOLIB and is on disk D10080, that DD card is:

    //TO DD DSNAME=TOLIB,UNIT=3330,VOL=SER=D10080,DISP=OLD

The Control Cards

For the first time we have two control cards. The first one is exactly the same as for copying the whole file:

    COPY INDD=FROM,OUTDD=TO

The second control card selects which members you want to have transferred. The action word is SELECT. The only parameter is MEMBER, and with it you give the names of the members you want copied over, separate their names with commas, and surround them with parentheses. If the members you want to copy are called PROGA and PROGB, you say:

    SELECT MEMBER=(PROGA,PROGB)

Both control cards together would then be:

    COPY INDD=FROM,OUTDD=TO
    SELECT MEMBER=(PROGA,PROGB)

On the other hand, you may want to copy over all the members except a few of them. Instead of having your control card name all those members you want copied over, there is a card you can use to name just the members you want excluded. Its action word is EXCLUDE, and it is used instead of the SELECT card. Again, the only parameter is MEMBER, and in the same format you give the names of the members you want excluded from the copy of the old file to the new file. To copy all the members except PROGX and PROGY, you say:

    EXCLUDE MEMBER=(PROGX,PROGY)

And both control cards would be:

    COPY INDD=FROM,OUTDD=TO
    EXCLUDE MEMBER=(PROGX,PROGY)

Rule 16. Copying the individual members from one partitioned file to another
using IEBCOPY requires four DD cards: two for the SYSUT3 and
SYSUT4 work files plus one for the OLD file from which you are
copying (DSN, UNIT, VOL=SER, DISP) and one for the OLD file to
which you are copying (DSN, UNIT, VOL=SER, DISP), both with any
DDnames. There are two control cards: COPY is the action word of
the first, with the parameters INDD and OUTDD; the action word for
the second is either SELECT or EXCLUDE, with the parameter
MEMBER giving the names of the members you want either included
or excluded from the copy operation.

And the whole job:

```
//COPYMEM           JOB     (accnt),NAME,MSGLEVEL=(1,1)
//STEP1             EXEC    PGM=IEBCOPY
//SYSPRINT          DD      SYSOUT=A
//FROM              DD      DSN=FROMLIB,UNIT=3330,VOL=SER=D10040,
//                          DISP=OLD
//TO                DD      DSN=TOLIB,UNIT=2314,VOL=SER=D10080,
//                          DISP=OLD
//SYSUT3            DD      UNIT=3330,SPACE=(TRK,5)
//SYSUT4            DD      UNIT=3330,SPACE=(TRK,5)
//SYSIN             DD      *
      COPY      INDD=FROM,OUTDD=TO
      SELECT    MEMBER=(PROGA,PROGB)
/*
//
```

COMPRESSING A PARTITIONED FILE

When a member moves out of a partitioned file, his room does not become
available again until the file is compressed, at which point all the rooms are
cleaned and the current members are moved to the beginning of the file. This
compressing is done by using IEBCOPY to copy the file to itself.

The DD Card

There is only one file, the file being compressed, and so only one DD card
is needed besides those for the SYSUT3 and SYSUT4 work files. (These work
files hold the members while the rooms are being cleaned.) The file already
exists, so the DD card for the OLD file on disk is used—file type number 1
(or 2 if it is cataloged). Any DD name can be used. If the file's name is
LIBFILE and it is on D10040, the card would simply be:

```
//LIB  DD  DSNAME=LIBFILE,UNIT=3330,VOL=SER=D10040,DISP=OLD
```

The Control Card

Again, the action word is COPY, and the parameters are INDD and OUTDD. If we want a file copied to itself (so it will be compressed), we have both INDD and OUTDD specifying the same name, the name of the DD card for our one file. If the DDname is LIB, the control card then is:

```
COPY  INDD=LIB,OUTDD=LIB
```

Rule 17. Compressing a partitioned file using IEBCOPY requires one DD card— besides those for the SYSUT3 and SYSUT4 work files—for the file being compressed, which is an OLD file on disk (DSN, UNIT, VOL=SER, DISP). The card can have any DDname and there's one control card. COPY is the action word. The two parameters INDD and OUTDD both specify the same name of the DD card for the file being compressed.

The whole job:

```
//COMPRESS       JOB      (accnt),NAME,MSGLEVEL=(1,1)
//STEP1          EXEC     PGM=IEBCOPY,REGION=100K
//SYSPRINT       DD       SYSOUT=A
//LIB            DD       DSNAME=LIBFILE,UNIT=3330,
//                        VOL=SER=D10040,DISP=OLD
//SYSUT3         DD       UNIT=3330,SPACE=(TRK,5)
//SYSUT4         DD       UNIT=3330,SPACE=(TRK,5)
//SYSIN          DD       *
        COPY   INDD=LIB,OUTDD=LIB
/*
//
```

Very important: You'll notice that there's an added parameter on the EXEC card, REGION=100K. This gives IEBCOPY more memory to work with, because without it, it has been known to foul up partitioned files. When compressing a partitioned file using IEBCOPY, add the parameter REGION=100K to the EXEC card.

We'll even make that a separate rule:

Rule 18. When compressing a partitioned file using IEBCOPY, add the parameter REGION=100K to the EXEC card.

QUESTIONS

1. Does IEBCOPY work with sequential or partitioned files?
2. IEBCOPY always needs two special DD cards in addition to those describing the input and output files it is to work with.

    a. What are the files for?

    b. What DDnames do they have to have?

    c. What two parameters are needed on both of them?

3. Give those two DD cards if we want each of them to have ten tracks of disk space.

4. *a.* When copying a whole partitioned file from one disk to another, how many DD cards do we need in addition to the SYSPRINT, SYSIN, and two work file DD cards?

    b. What DDnames do they have to have?

5. *a.* The input file describes an old file on disk; what parameters does it need if not cataloged?

    b. What if it is cataloged?

    c. What is its DISP parameter?

6. The output file describes a new file on disk.

    a. What parameters does its DD card need?

    b. What would its DISP parameter be?

    c. What would its SPACE parameter look like if we want to reserve 100 tracks and anticipate there will not be more than 90 members?

    d. Why is the second number on the SPACE parameter needed to create a partitioned file?

7. Give the two DD cards (for the input and output disk files) if we are copying a partitioned file called PARTFILE on disk D10020 to disk D10010. (It will have the same name on the new disk and will have 50 tracks; we anticipate that not more than 120 members will be in it.)

8. Give the following information for the control card used in copying a whole partitioned file from one disk to another:

    a. What is the action word?

    b. What are the two parameters?

    c. Give the control card needed if the DDnames of the input and output files are OLDISK and NEWDISK, respectively.

9. When copying individual members from one partitioned file to another, what is the DISP parameter on the DD card describing the following:

    a. The input file.

    b. The output file.

    c. What four parameters are needed on each of these DD cards if the files are not cataloged?

10. *a.* How many control cards are needed for copying individual members?

    b. What is the action word on the first?

    c. What are the two parameters on the first?

    d. What two possible action words can be on the second?

    e. What parameter is needed on the second?

11. Which action word would you use on the second control card in these
    instances:
    a. If you were copying two members of a 50-member file.
    b. If you were copying 48 members of a 50-member file.
12. Give the two control cards needed to copy two members, MEM1 and
    MEM2; assume the DD names of the cards describing the input and
    output files are FROMDISK and TODISK, respectively.
13. When compressing a partitioned file, how many DD cards are needed be-
    sides those for the SYSPRINT, SYSIN, and the two work space files?
14. Give the following information for the control card needed to compress
    a file:
    a. What action word is needed?
    b. What two parameters are needed?
    c. What can be said about the DD cards referred to by these two param-
       eters?
15. What special parameter must go on the JOB card when compressing a
    partitioned file?

BREATHER

Halfway through our eight Utilities, you can see that there are a lot of rules
that have to be either remembered or constantly looked up. For this reason, the
rules will be listed in the back. Often, however, understanding the concepts behind the rules helps a great deal. When you want to use a Utility, just ask yourself these two questions:

1. How many and what kinds of files are involved (for the DD cards).
2. What information about the files and the action does the Utility need
   to know (for the control card).

8 IEHMOVE

To some extent, IEHMOVE has a bad reputation. Reading the description of its many options and rules in the IBM Utilities Manual is like trudging through a tropical rain forest. And its occasional unpredictability has given it the nickname of IEHMOOD.

But our simple rules will make the going safe and easy. We will limit ourselves to IEHMOVE's most common and useful function: taking partitioned files on disk and backing them up onto tape, and then restoring them from the backup tapes. You might recall that IEHDASDR can back up and restore entire disk packs. An important distinction is that IEHMOVE just backs up and restores individual partitioned files on disks. Backing up the partitioned file onto tape is called unloading the file.

THE WORK FILE

IEHMOVE always requires a special DD card that supplies it with some disk work space. The name of the DD card is SYSUT1, and the only two parameters on it are UNIT and SPACE, since it is a temporary disk file (file type number 7). For the SPACE parameter, give 30 tracks (of 3330 space) for every 800 members in your partitioned file. Since most partitioned files have fewer members than that, the entire DD card would look like this:

```
//SYSUT1   DD   UNIT=3330,SPACE=(TRK,30)
```

Rule 19. IEHMOVE needs a special DD card for disk work space that looks like this: //SYSUT1   DD   UNIT=3330,SPACE=(TRK,30). More disk space is needed in the rare instances when the partitioned file you are working with has over 800 members.

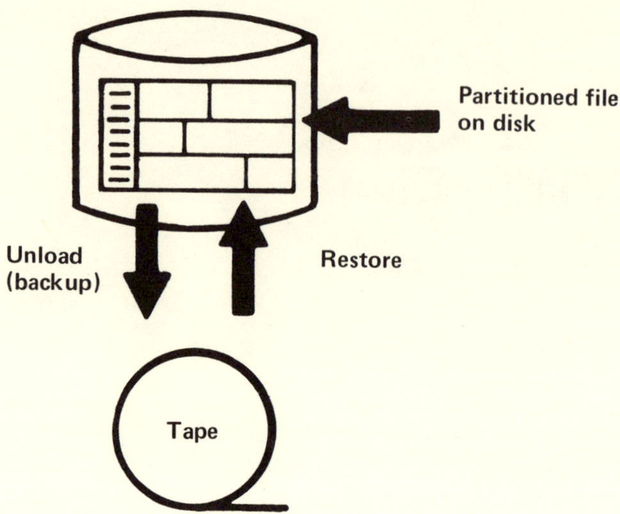

Fig. 8.1.   IEHMOVE can unload a partitioned file to a backup tape and then
restore the partitioned file back to disk from the backup tape.

THE TWO DD CARDS

We use IEHMOVE to move a partitioned file from disk onto a tape (unloading), or from tape back onto the disk (restoring). In each case, two DD
cards are needed, one for disk and one for tape. They can have any DDname.
While unloading or restoring, the DD card for the disk specifies the entire
pack (file type number 8), with the UNIT, VOL=SER, and DISP=OLD parameters.
Example:

    //DISK   DD   UNIT=3330,VOL=SER=D10040,DISP=OLD

The DD card for the tape differs slightly, depending on whether you are
unloading or restoring the partitioned file. If you are unloading the partitioned
file from the disk onto a tape, the DD card for the tape is for a new file on
tape (file type 6), with DSNAME, UNIT, and DISP=(NEW,KEEP). Example:

    //TAPE   DD   DSN=TAPE,UNIT=3400-3,DISP=(NEW,KEEP)

However, if you are restoring from the tape back onto the disk, you are using
an old file on tape (file type 3), and need the DSN, UNIT, VOL=SER, and
DISP=OLD parameters. For example, if the tape is 000040:

    //TAPE   DD   DSN=TAPE,UNIT=3400-3,VOL=SER=000040,DISP=OLD

Rule 20. When using IEHMOVE to move a partitioned file from disk onto

tape (unloading) or from the tape back onto the disk (restoring),
two DD cards are needed, one for disk and one for tape. They can
have any DDnames. The one for the disk specifies a whole pack
(UNIT, VOL, DISP). The DD card for the tape specifies a new file on
tape (DSN, UNIT, DISP=(NEW,KEEP)) when unloading the file to tape,
and specifies an old file on tape (DSN, UNIT, VOL, DISP=OLD) when
restoring.

Examples: When unloading the partitioned file from disk D10040 to a scratch
tape:

```
//DISK   DD   UNIT=3330,VOL=SER=D10040,DISP=OLD
//TAPE   DD   DSN=TAPE,UNIT=3400-3,DISP=(NEW,KEEP)
```

When subsequently restoring the file from tape 000040 back onto disk
D10040:

```
//DISK   DD   UNIT=3330,VOL=SER=D10040,DISP=OLD
//TAPE   DD   DSN=TAPE,UNIT=3400-3,VOL=SER=000040,DISP=OLD
```

Important note: Before restoring the partitioned file back onto the disk,
you must scratch (remove) or rename the partitioned file on the disk if it is
still there.

THE CONTROL CARD

There is one control card, and COPY is the action word. There are three
parameters that are used whether you are unloading or restoring:

```
PDS=   FROM=   TO=
```

Now, PDS specifies the DSNAME of the partitioned file—for example,
PDS=PARTFILE. The FROM and TO parameters specify the unit type and volume serial numbers of the devices we are moving from or to—for example,
FROM=3330=D10040. The only unusual point is that when unloading the file
to tape, we say the tape's volume serial number is SCRTCH; since we don't
want to name a specific tape, we'd rather let the system mount a scratch tape
for us.

So far, assuming our partitioned file is named PARTFILE and is on disk
D10040, the control card looks like this:
when unloading:

```
COPY   PDS=PARTFILE,FROM=3330=D10040,TO=3400-3=SCRTCH
```

when restoring from tape 000040

```
COPY   PDS=PARTFILE,FROM=3400-3=000040,TO=3330=D10040
```

In addition, there are two more parameters, TODD and FROMDD, which both refer to the name of the DD card for the tape. We use TODD when unloading *to* tape, and FROMDD when restoring *from* tape. For example, if the DD card for tape is named TAPE, this parameter would be TODD=TAPE when unloading and FROMDD=TAPE when restoring.

So our complete control card when unloading a partitioned file from disk to tape is:

```
COPY   PDS=PARTFILE,FROM=3330=D10040,TO=3400-3=SCRTCH,TODD=TAPE
```

When restoring, our control card is:

```
COPY   PDS=PARTFILE,FROM=3400-3=000040,TO=3330=D10040,              C
       FROMDD=TAPE
```

Rule 21. IEHMOVE needs one control card, and COPY is the action word. Now, PDS gives the name of the partitioned file. And FROM and TO specify the unit type and volume serial numbers of the devices we are moving the file from and to (when unloading, say TO=3400-3=SCRTCH). We name the DD card for the tape with TODD when unloading to tape and FROMDD when restoring from tape.

The whole job, when unloading, is as follows:

```
//UNLDPDS    JOB     (accnt),NAME,MSGLEVEL=(1,1)
//STEP1      EXEC    PGM=IEHMOVE
//SYSPRINT   DD      SYSOUT=A
//SYSUT1     DD      UNIT=3330,SPACE=(TRK,30)
//DISK       DD      UNIT=3330,VOL=SER=D10040,DISP=OLD
//TAPE       DD      DSN=TAPE,UNIT=3400-3,DISP=(NEW,KEEP)
//SYSIN      DD      *
        COPY  PDS=PARTFILE,FROM=3330=D10040,TO=3400-3=SCRTCH,        C
              TODD=TAPE
/*
//
```

When restoring the partitioned file to disk, the whole job is:

```
//RSTRPDS    JOB     (accnt),NAME,MSGLEVEL=(1,1)
//STEP1      EXEC    PGM=IEHMOVE
//SYSPRINT   DD      SYSOUT=A
//SYSUT1     DD      UNIT=3330,SPACE=(TRK,30)
//DISK       DD      UNIT=3330,VOL=SER=D10040,DISP=OLD
//TAPE       DD      DSN=TAPE,UNIT=3400-3,VOL=SER=000040,DISP=OLD
//SYSIN      DD      *
```

```
          COPY      PDS=PARTFILE,FROM=3400-3=000040,TO=3330=D10040,        C
    /*              FROMDD=TAPE
    //
```

QUESTIONS

1. IEHDASDR can back up and restore an entire disk pack. What type of file (discussed here) can IEHMOVE back up and restore?
2. When using IEHMOVE, what is the other term used to describe the process of backing up a file?
3. IEHMOVE always needs a special DD card to describe temporary work space.
    a. What is its DDname?
    b. What two parameters are needed?
    c. If you were working with a partitioned file with 100 members, how much 3330 disk space would be required?
    d. Show the entire DD card.
4. What two types of I/O devices are involved in the following:
    a. Unloading a partitioned file.
    b. Restoring a partitioned file.
5. Which is the input device and which is the output device in these circumstances:
    a. Unloading a partitioned file.
    b. Restoring a partitioned file.
6. *a.* In either case, how many DD cards are required besides those for SYSPRINT, SYSUT1, and SYSIN?
    b. What do their DDnames have to be?
7. Is the DD card for the disk partitioned file the same for unloading and restoring the partitioned file?
8. What three parameters are needed on it?
9. Give the entire DD card if we are using disk D10020 for the following:
    a. Unloading a partitioned file *from* it.
    b. Restoring a partitioned file *to* it.
10. *a.* In the two cases of unloading or restoring a partitioned file, in which case is the tape file new?
    b. In which case is the file old?
11. *a.* What would the DISP parameter be when the tape file is new?
    b. What would it be when the tape file is old?
12. *a.* When unloading the file to a new tape, do we have to give a specific volume serial number?
    b. Why?

    c. How about in the case of restoring the file from tape?

13.   *a.* What three parameters are needed for the tape DD card when unloading the file to tape?

    b. Give the whole DD card for the tape file when unloading a file to tape.

14.   *a.* What four parameters are needed for the tape DD card when restoring a file from tape?

    b. Give such a DD card when restoring a file from tape 000020.

15.   *a.* Will the restore operation work if IEHMOVE finds a partitioned file with the same name as the one being restored on the disk pack?

    b. If there is such an old file on the disk to which you want to restore, what two things can be done to this old file to allow a restore to take place.

16.   How many control cards are needed to unload or restore a partitioned file?

17.   What is the action word?

18.   What parameter gives the DSNAME of the file?

19.   What two parameters specify unit types and volume serial numbers?

20.   Which of these two parameters specifies the following:

    a. Input.

    b. Output.

21.   If we are unloading a partitioned file named FILE1 from disk D10025 to a scratch tape that the system has mounted, give the following:

    a. PDS parameter.

    b. FROM parameter.

    c. TO parameter.

22.   If we are restoring the same partitioned file to the disk it came from, and the backup tape is 000025, give the following:

    a. PDS parameter.

    b. FROM parameter.

    c. TO parameter.

23.   The other control card parameters are FROMDD and TODD. Which one of the following do they always refer to:

    a. Disk file.

    b. Tape file.

24.   What is true about the parameter FROMDD and TODD?

    a. They are always found together on the same control card.

    b. One or the other must be used on any control card, but not both.

25.   Which of these two parameters is used when the tape file is the following:

    a. Output.

    b. Input.

26. If a DD card for a tape file is named **TAPE**, give the following that would be used to refer to it:
    a. FROMDD parameter
    b. TODD parameter
27. In the following examples, the DD card for the tape file is named **TAPE**. Give the entire control card for the following:
    a. Unloading a partitioned file named **PARTFILE** from disk D10080 to a scratch tape.
    b. Restoring **PARTFILE** back to disk D10080 from tape 000085, to which it was previously unloaded.

9 IEHPROGM

This Utility can do three things: catalog and uncatalog, rename a file or member, and scratch a file, a member, or a whole pack. For any of these functions, IEHPROGM always needs one type of DD card.

THE DD CARD

This DD card describes the one disk pack or drum you are working with. Use the type of DD card that refers to the whole pack, which is file type number 8 (UNIT, VOL, DISP). Use any DDname. If you are cataloging or uncataloging, this would be the system pack or drum that holds the catalog. For instance, if the catalog is on a 2305 drum with the volume serial number DD2305, the DD card would be:

```
//DRUM   DD   UNIT=2305,VOL=SER=DD2305,DISP=OLD
```

Or if you're renaming or scratching a file that is on disk pack D10040, the DD card would be:

```
//DISK   DD   UNIT=3330,VOL=SER=D10040,DISP=OLD
```

Rule 22. IEHPROGM needs one DD card for the disk or drum you are working with, specifying the whole pack (UNIT, VOL, DISP).

THE CONTROL CARDS

The control cards are different for each of the things IEHPROGM can do.

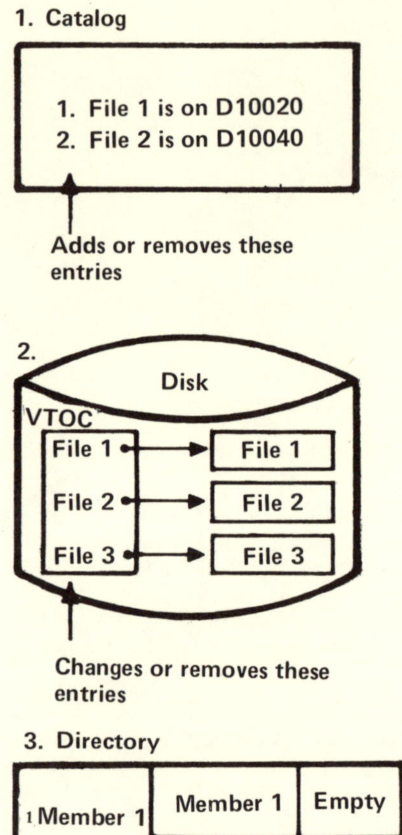

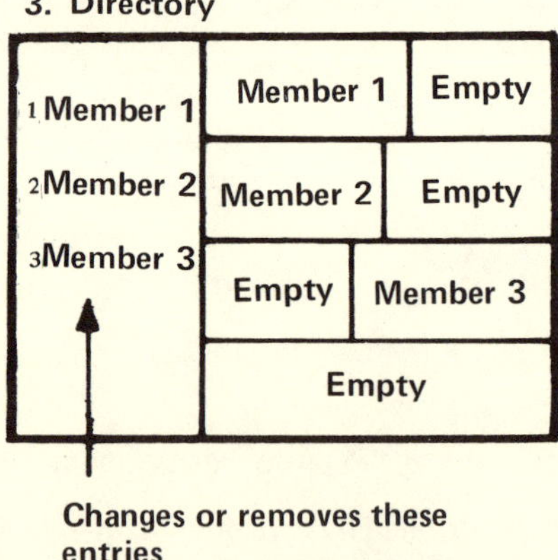

Fig. 9.1. IEHPROGM can: (1) catalog or uncatalog; (2) rename or scratch files on a disk pack by changing the names or removing the entries in the VTOC; and (3) rename or scratch members of a partitioned file by changing the names or removing the entries in the directory.

CATALOGING A FILE

The catalog is a list of the names of important files; alongside each name
is the volume serial number of the tape or disk that the file is on. To catalog a
file means adding the file's name and volume serial number to this list.

On the control card the action word is CATLG. There are two parameters:
DSNAME, which specifies the name of the file you want cataloged; and VOL,
which gives the unit type and volume serial number of the disk or tape the
file is on. For example, if you want to catalog the file named FILE, which is
on disk D10040, the control card is:

```
CATLG   DSNAME=FILE,VOL=3330=D10040
```

Rule 23. Cataloging a file using IEHPROGM requires one control card, and
         CATLG is the action word. The two parameters are: DSNAME, giving
         the name of the file; and VOL, giving the unit type and volume serial
         number of the disk or tape that the file is on.

This, then, is the whole job. Remember, the DD card is for the disk or drum
the catalog is on, because that's the file you are working with:

```
//CATLG          JOB      (accnt),NAME,MSGLEVEL=(1,1)
//STEP1          EXEC     PGM=IEHPROGM
//SYSPRINT       DD       SYSOUT=A
//DRUM           DD       UNIT=2305,VOL=SER=DD2305,DISP=OLD
//SYSIN          DD       *
        CATLG  DSNAME=FILE,VOL=3330=D10040
/*
//
```

UNCATALOGING A FILE

This does just the reverse—namely, takes the name of the file and its volume
serial number off the catalog. All you have to do is give the file's name. The
action word is UNCATLG. The one parameter is DSNAME, where you give the
file's name. To uncatalog the file named FILE, just say:

```
UNCATLG   DSNAME=FILE
```

Rule 24. Uncataloging a file using IEHPROGM requires one control card, and
         UNCATLG is the action word. The one parameter is DSNAME, giving
         the name of the file to be uncataloged.

If the catalog is on the drum DD2305, the whole job is:

```
//UNCATLG        JOB      (accnt),NAME,MSGLEVEL=(1,1)
```

```
//STEP1            EXEC   PGM=IEHPROGM
//SYSPRINT         DD     SYSOUT=A
//DRUM             DD     UNIT=2305,VOL=SER=DD2305,DISP=OLD
//SYSIN            DD     *
    UNCATLG   DSNAME=FILE
/*
//
```

RENAMING A FILE

Every file has a name, and this Utility can change it. On the control card, the action word is RENAME. And then there are three parameters:

DSNAME. This specifies the file's current name. For example, if the file is now called LIB, you say DSNAME=LIB.

VOL. Here you give the unit type and volume serial number of the disk pack that contains the file. If the file is on disk D10040, you say VOL=3330=D10040.

NEWNAME. This specifies the new name, the one you want the file's current name changed to. If, from now on, you want this file referred to by name LIBA, you say NEWNAME=LIBA.

```
    RENAME   DSNAME=LIB,VOL=3330=D10040,NEWNAME=LIBA
```

Rule 25. Renaming a file using IEHPROGM requires one control card, and RENAME is the action word. The parameters are: DSNAME, giving the file's current name; VOL, giving the unit type and volume serial number of the pack that the file is on; and NEWNAME, specifying the new name you want to give to the file.

And the whole job:

```
//RENAME           JOB    (accnt),NAME,MSGLEVEL=(1,1)
//STEP1            EXEC   PGM=IEHPROGM
//SYSPRINT         DD     SYSOUT=A
//DISK             DD     UNIT=3330,VOL=SER=D10040,DISP=OLD
//SYSIN            DD     *
    RENAME   DSNAME=LIB,VOL=3330=D10040,NEWNAME=LIBA
/*
//
```

RENAMING A MEMBER OF A PARTITIONED FILE

At the beginning of a partitioned file is a directory that lists the names of all the members in the file. Each member's name can be changed using IEHPROGM. The control card is slightly different, because now we're renaming a single member and not the whole file. Again, RENAME is the action word. These are the four parameters:

DSNAME. This, as before, gives the name of the whole partitioned file that the member is in. If the member is in a partitioned file called LIB, you say DSNAME=LIB.

VOL. This is the same, too, giving the unit type and volume serial number of the pack the file is on. If the partitioned file LIB is on D10040, then say VOL=3330=D10040.

MEMBER. This is the new parameter that specifies the member you want renamed. To rename the member called MEM, just say MEMBER=MEM.

NEWNAME. And here you specify the new name you want given to the member. If you say NEWNAME=MEMA, that means the member's name will be changed to MEMA. The name of the whole partitioned file is left unchanged. So, for this example, which changes MEM's name to MEMA, the control card is:

```
     RENAME   DSNAME=LIB,VOL=3330=D10040,MEMBER=MEM,            C
              NEWNAME=MEMA
```

As you can see, once the parameter MEMBER is added, you are working with individual members and not with the whole file.

Rule 26. Renaming a member of a partitioned file using IEHPROGM requires one control card, and RENAME is the action word. The parameters are: DSNAME, giving the name of the whole partitioned file; VOL, with the unit type and volume serial number of the pack that the file is on; MEMBER, giving the name of the member to be renamed; and NEWNAME, which specifies what you want the member's new name to be.

The whole job:

```
//RENAMEM          JOB      (accnt),NAME,MSGLEVEL=(1,1)
//STEP1            EXEC     PGM=IEHPROGM
//SYSPRINT         DD       SYSOUT=A
//DISK             DD       UNIT=3330,VOL=SER=D10040,DISP=OLD
//SYSIN            DD       *
          RENAME   DSNAME=LIB,VOL=3330=D10040,MEMBER=MEM,            C
                   NEWNAME=MEMA
/*
//
```

SCRATCHING A FILE

To scratch a file means deleting it from the disk pack it's on. For the control card, SCRATCH is the action word, and there are two parameters:

DSNAME. This specifies the file you want to scratch.

VOL. This gives the number of the disk pack it's on.

So the control card to scratch the file SOMEFILE off disk D10040 would look like:

    SCRATCH   DSNAME=SOMEFILE,VOL=3330=D10040

Note: When a file is created, it can be specified that the file is not to be scratched until a certain date, called the expiration date. So the above control card would not delete a file whose expiration date had not been reached yet. A message would come back, saying, "The file can't be scratched yet." But if you want to scratch the file anyway, in spite of its expiration date, you can add another parameter to the control card, PURGE!

    SCRATCH   DSNAME=SOMEFILE,VOL=3330=D10040,PURGE

This says to delete SOMEFILE even if it's expiration date has not come yet.

Rule 27. Scratching a file using IEHPROGM requires one control card, and SCRATCH is the action word. The parameters are: DSNAME, naming the file you want scratched; and VOL, giving the unit type and number of the pack it's on; the parameter PURGE can be added if the file is to be scratched before its expiration date.

An example of a whole job (without PURGE):

```
//SRCHFILE        JOB     (accnt),NAME,MSGLEVEL=(1,1)
//STEP1           EXEC    PGM=IEHPROGM
//SYSPRINT        DD      SYSOUT=A
//DISK            DD      UNIT=3330,VOL=SER=D10040,DISP=OLD
//SYSIN           DD      *
     SCRATCH    DSNAME=SOMEFILE,VOL=3330=D10040
/*
//
```

SCRATCHING A MEMBER OF A PARTITIONED FILE

Here just one member of a partitioned file is deleted, leaving the rest of the members alone. The control card is similar to the one for scratching a whole file, with SCRATCH as the action word and DSNAME and VOL as the parameters, but now one parameter is added:

MEMBER. This names the member you want scratched.

If the control card is—

    SCRATCH   DSNAME=SOMEFILE,VOL=3330=D10040,MEMBER=SOMEMEM

—the member SOMEMEM would be deleted from the partitioned file SOMEMFILE, which is on pack D10040.

Rule 28. Scratching a member of a partitioned file using IEHPROGM requires
one control card, and SCRATCH is the action word. The parameters
are: DSNAME, giving the name of the partitioned file; VOL, telling
the unit type and which pack the file is on; and MEMBER, naming
the member to be scratched.

The whole job:

```
//SRCHMEM          JOB     (accnt),NAME,MSGLEVEL=(1,1)
//STEP1            EXEC    PGM=IEHPROGM
//SYSPRINT         DD      SYSOUT=A
//DISK             DD      UNIT=3330,VOL=SER=D10040,DISP=OLD
//SYSIN            DD      *
     SCRATCH   DSNAME=SOMEFILE,VOL=3330=D10040,MEMBER=SOMEMEM
/*
//
```

SCRATCHING ALL THE FILES ON A DISK PACK

You can also ask IEHPROGM to scratch all the files on a disk pack. For
this control card, SCRATCH is still the action word. You tell it to scratch all
the files with a new parameter, VTOC, which has no equal sign. The second
parameter is VOL, telling from which pack the files should be scratched. For
example, the control card to scratch all the files on disk D10040 would look
like this:

```
SCRATCH   VTOC,VOL=3330=D10040
```

Note: Again, this control card as it is would leave alone files that had not
yet reached their expiration dates. Therefore, to scratch all the files, including
those that have not yet expired, use the word PURGE. For example:

```
SCRATCH   VTOC,VOL=3330=D10040,PURGE
```

Rule 29. Scratching all the files on a disk pack using IEHPROGM requires one
control card, and SCRATCH is the action word. The parameters are:
VTOC, with no equal sign; and VOL, giving the number of the pack to
be cleaned out; the parameter PURGE can be added to scratch files
that haven't yet expired.

Here is an example of such a job (using PURGE so that we get a completely
clean pack):

```
//SRCHVTOC         JOB     (accnt),NAME,MSGLEVEL=(1,1)
//STEP1            EXEC    PGM=IEHPROGM
//SYSPRINT         DD      SYSOUT=A
```

```
//DISK              DD      UNIT=3330,VOL=SER=D10040,DISP=OLD
//SYSIN             DD      *
       SCRATCH   VTOC,VOL=3330=D10040,PURGE
/*
//
```

As you can see, each function of IEHPROGM is very easy to use. It gets complicated only because it can do so many things.

QUESTIONS

1. What are the two things that IEHPROGM can do to the following:
   a. The catalog.
   b. Volume table of contents of a disk.
   c. Directory of a partitioned file.
2. IEHPROGM always needs only one DD card in addition to the SYSPRINT and SYSIN DD cards.
   a. What does its DDname have to be?
   b. What parameters are needed on the DD card?
   c. Why isn't the DSNAME parameter needed?
3. What is the action word needed for the following IEHPROGM operations:
   a. Giving a member of a partitioned file a new name.
   b. Removing an entry in the catalog for a file.
   c. Removing an entry in the VTOC for a file.
   d. Adding an entry in the catalog for a file.
4. What parameters are needed on the control card for the following operations:
   a. Uncataloging a file.
   b. Cataloging a file.
   c. Renaming a file.
   d. Renaming a member.
5. To catalog a file, you need the VOL parameter on the control card. Why do you suppose it is not needed for uncataloging a file?
6. Give the whole control card for the following operations:
   a. Cataloging a file named FILEONE, which is on tape 002000.
   b. Uncataloging the file named FILEONE.
   c. Renaming the file DSKFILE1 on disk D10020 to DSKFILE2.
   d. Renaming a member of a file PARTFILE on disk D10020 from OLD to NEW.
7. Let's say we have a file that exists on cards, disk, and tape.

a. Which of them can be cataloged?

b. Which of them can be renamed?

c. Which of them can be scratched?

8. In a rename operation, which parameter on the control card can do the following:

    a. Give the name to be changed to.

    b. Indicate that not the whole file, but just a member of the file, is to be renamed.

9. What would happen if you meant to rename a member of a file, but forgot the parameter MEMBER?

10. What would happen if you meant to scratch just a member of a file, but left out the parameter MEMBER?

11. *a.* If you are cataloging a file on disk D10020 and the catalog is on disk D10040, to which disk does the DD card refer?

    b. To which disk does the control card refer?

12. When scratching a file or a whole pack, what parameter is added if you want the file scratched even if its expiration date has not yet passed?

13. What parameter indicates that you want all the files on a disk pack scratched?

14. If the expiration date of a partitioned file has not yet passed, and you want to scratch a member without using the parameter PURGE, will the member be scratched?

15. What parameter is on every IEHPROGM control card except for:

    a. Uncataloging a file.

    b. The scratch VTOC operation.

16. Give the control card to do the following:

    a. Scratch a file named FILEA on disk D10010 only if its expiration date has not passed.

    b. Scratch the above file even if the expiration date has not passed.

    c. Scratch a member of FILEB on D10005 called MEMA.

    d. Scratch only those files on disk D10005 whose expiration dates have passed.

    e. Scratch all the files on disk D10005 even if their expiration dates have not passed.

10 IEBPTPCH

Sometimes we may need to see the information that is actually out there on the disks and tapes we use. Then we can use IEBPTPCH, which, as its name implies, can print out on paper or punch out on cards the information on a disk or a tape. This Utility can print and punch partitioned and sequential files residing on disk and tape. But we will focus on just one of its most common functions—printing out a partitioned card image file on disk. A card image file, as you remember, is one whose information is exactly what was on the cards that were transferred over intact to the file.

Two terms may be helpful here. A card has 80 columns of letters and numbers, and when on the disk, these 80 columns of information make up what is called a *record*. A whole record can be divided up into little sections of information called *fields*. The best known card image file is SYS1.PROCLIB, which contains on disk the images of frequently used Job Control Language. Now let's talk about the DD cards needed for IEBPTPCH.

The DD Cards

There are two DD cards, one for the disk file from which you are printing, the other for where you are printing to—the printer itself. Each DD card must have the specific name that IEBPTPCH expects it to have. The name of the DD card describing the disk file must be SYSUT1, and the name of the DD card describing the printer must be SYSUT2.

Looking back at the JCL section, we see that the disk file we want to look at is an old file on disk. The DD card would be for file type number 1 if it is uncataloged (DSN, UNIT, VOL, DISP), or for file type number 2 if it is cataloged (just DSN and DISP). For discussion's sake, let us say that the file we want to print out is SYS1.PROCLIB and that it is cataloged. Then the first DD card would be:

```
//SYSUT1   DD   DSNAME=SYS1.PROCLIB,DISP=SHR
```

Note that we say DISP=SHR, indicating that SYS1.PROCLIB, a heavily used file, can be shared with other programs in the system. We would say DISP=OLD in reference to a file only when we are changing its contents and need to lock out other people from using it until we are done. Here, since we are only reading from it, we say DISP=SHR.

1. Partitioned card image file

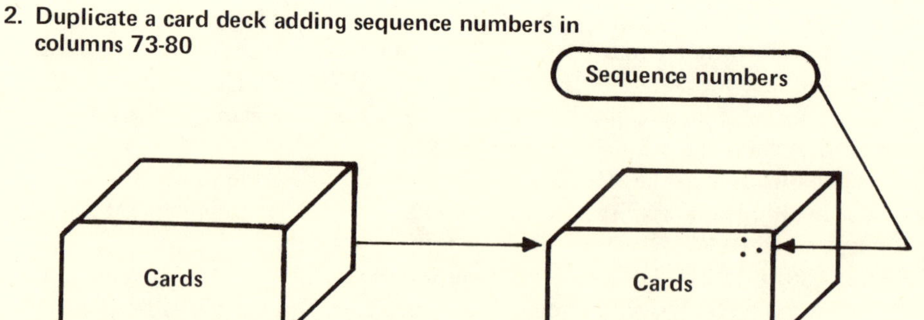

2. Duplicate a card deck adding sequence numbers in columns 73-80

Fig. 10.1.   IEBPTPCH can print or punch out members of partitioned card image files or duplicate a card deck, adding sequence numbers.

The second DD card is always the same: it has to have the name SYSUT2, and it always refers to the printer, which is done by saying SYSOUT=A. So it always looks like this:

```
//SYSUT2  DD   SYSOUT=A
```

The two DD cards together are:

```
//SYSUT1   DD   DSNAME=SYS1.PROCLIB,DISP=SHR
//SYSUT2   DD   SYSOUT=A
```

Rule 30. IEBPTPCH needs two DD cards. The first, which must have the name SYSUT1, describes the file you are printing from (often a cataloged partitioned file on disk, needing DSN and DISP). The second DD card, which must have the name SYSUT2, describes the printer (SYSOUT=A).

The Control Cards

IEBPTPCH uses three kinds of control cards, each identified by their action words—PRINT, MEMBER, and RECORD. The card that always comes first is the PRINT card. Its action word is PRINT, saying that you want to print the file. We'll talk about its parameters in a second.

The MEMBER card is the second card, and its action word is MEMBER. With its one parameter, NAME, you identify the specific member you want to print. To print the member called WTR, just say:

```
MEMBER   NAME=WTR
```

The third card is the RECORD card, with RECORD as its action word. It describes the length of the record with its one parameter, FIELD. Since the cards in card image files are always 80 columns long, then for a partitioned card image file (which is our example), the RECORD card always looks like this:

```
RECORD   FIELD=(80)
```

The MEMBER and RECORD cards are used in pairs, one pair for every member you want printed. The RECORD card always comes after the MEMBER card in a pair. For example, to print two members, WTR and RDR, the two pairs of cards look alike:

```
MEMBER   NAME=WTR
RECORD   FIELD=(80)
MEMBER   NAME=RDR
RECORD   FIELD=(80)
```

Now let's come back to the first card, the PRINT card. It has three parameters:

TYPORG. This stands for type of organization of the file. Since it is partitioned organization in our example, we say TYPORG=PO.

MAXNAME. This specifies the maximum number of MEMBER cards we are using, usually the same as the number of members we are printing out (NAME is the parameter on the MEMBER card). If we are printing two members, we say: MAXNAME=2.

MAXFLDS. This specifies the number of RECORD cards we are using (FIELD is the parameter on the RECORD card). If two RECORD cards, then say: MAXFLDS=2.

All the control cards needed to print out the members WTR and RDR are now:

```
PRINT      TYPORG=PO,MAXNAME=2,MAXFLDS=2
MEMBER     NAME=WTR
RECORD     FIELD=(80)
MEMBER     NAME=RDR
RECORD     FIELD=(80)
```

Rule 31. Printing out individual members of a partitioned card image file using IEBPTPCH requires three types of control cards. On the first card, PRINT is the action word. Its three parameters are: TYPORG=PO, specifying partitioned organization of the file; MAXNAME, giving the number of MEMBER cards that follow; and MAXFLDS, giving the number of RECORD cards that follow. After that comes a pair of cards for every member to be printed. MEMBER is the action word on the first card of each pair; its parameter, NAME, names the member to be printed. RECORD is the action word on the second card of each pair, and its parameter, FIELD, gives the length of the record (usually FIELD=(80)).

An example of the job:

```
//PRINTMEM        JOB     (accnt),NAME,MSGLEVEL=(1,1)
//STEP1           EXEC    PGM=IEBPTPCH
//SYSPRINT        DD      SYSOUT=A
//SYSUT1          DD      DSNAME=SYS1,PROCLIB,DISP=SHR
//SYSUT2          DD      SYSOUT=A
//SYSIN           DD      *
   PRINT      TYPORG=PO,MAXNAME=2,MAXFLDS=2
   MEMBER     NAME=WTR
   RECORD     FIELD=(80)
   MEMBER     NAME=RDR
   RECORD     FIELD=(80)
/*
//
```

We can be thankful that there is a simple way of saying that all the members of the file are to be printed, without having to name every member. For this case, you don't have to put in any MEMBER cards, and only one RECORD card is needed. It looks like this:

```
PRINT     TYPORG=PO,MAXFLDS=1
RECORD    FIELD=(80)
```

This prints the whole file with all its members. The MAXNAME parameter on the PRINT card is left out because there are *no* MEMBER cards that follow. Let's make this a separate rule:

Rule 32. Printing all the members of a partitioned card image file using IEBPTPCH requires two control cards. On the first card, PRINT is the action word. Its parameters are: TYPORG=PO, specifying partitioned organization; and MAXFLDS=1, saying that one RECORD card follows. RECORD is the action word of the second card, and its parameter is FIELD=(80), specifying the length of each record.

The job looks like this:

```
//PRINTLIB        JOB     (accnt),NAME,MSGLEVEL=(1,1)
//STEP1           EXEC    PGM=IEBPTPCH
//SYSPRINT        DD      SYSOUT=A
//SYSUT1          DD      DSN=SYS1.PROCLIB,DISP=SHR
//SYSUT2          DD      SYSOUT=A
//SYSIN           DD      *
   PRINT          TYPORG=PO,MAXFLDS=1
   RECORD         FIELD=(80)
/*
//
```

As its name implies, IEBPTPCH (print/punch) can also be used to punch out the members of a partitioned card image file. The process is exactly the same as printing, except for two small differences.

1. The SYSUT2 DD card, instead of referring to the printer, refers to the card punch (SYSOUT=B), so it looks like this:

```
//SYSUT2  DD  SYSOUT=B
```

2. The action word on the first control card, instead of being PRINT, is PUNCH.

The cards necessary to punch out the members named WTR and RDR from the partitioned file SYS1.PROCLIB would look very similar to those you'd use to print them. The control cards are:

```
PUNCH      TYPORG=PO,MAXNAME=2,MAXFLDS=2
MEMBER     NAME=WTR
RECORD     FIELD=(80)
MEMBER     NAME=RDR
RECORD     FIELD=(80)
```

And the whole job:

```
//PUNCHMEM      JOB      (accnt),NAME,MSGLEVEL=(1,1)
//STEP1         EXEC     PGM=IEBPTPCH
//SYSPRINT      DD       SYSOUT=A
//SYSUT1        DD       DSNAME=SYS1.PROCLIB,DISP=SHR
//SYSUT2        DD       SYSOUT=B
//SYSIN         DD       *
     PUNCH      TYPORG=PO,MAXNAME=2,MAXFLDS=2
     MEMBER     NAME=WTR
     RECORD     FIELD=(80)
     MEMBER     NAME=RDR
     RECORD     FIELD=(80)
/*
//
```

Rule 33. Punching out members of a partitioned card image file using
IEBPTPCH involves the same DD cards and control cards used for
printing the members, except that the SYSUT2 (output) DD card
must refer to the card punch (SYSOUT=B), and the action word on
the first control card is PUNCH.

NEW SEQUENCE NUMBERS

Before we leave IEBPTPCH, I want to share with you a useful, but less
known application of IEBPTPCH. When testing a program, programmers
sometimes have it on punched cards. They usually use columns 73–80 for
sequence numbers, so that if the card deck falls, the cards can be easily sorted
to get them back in order. But let's say that you finish the program and then
realize that with all the changes you've made, the sequence numbers are not
in order anymore. IEBPTPCH can then be used to punch out a new deck with
new sequence numbers. This is how to do it.

There are still two DD cards, SYSUT1 and SYSUT2, but they look slightly
odd. The SYSUT1 DD card here defines your old card deck, because that's
what IEBPTPCH has to read in as input in order to duplicate it. The DD
card looks like this:

```
//SYSUT1   DD   *
```

        [*old card deck goes here*]

```
/*
```

That's right, the SYSUT1 DD card is followed by your old card deck. As you
know, the /* card is put after all card decks and serves to tell that we've
reached the end of the card deck.

The SYSUT2 card refers to the card punch, because that's going to be your
output, a new punched deck. It looks like this:

```
//SYSUT2   DD   SYSOUT=B
```

The two DD cards together are as follows:

```
//SYSUT1   DD   *
```

        [*old card deck*]

```
/*
//SYSUT2   DD   SYSOUT=B
```

There are two control cards. Let's get the second one over with first. It looks
like this:

```
RECORD   FIELD=(72)
```

We've come upon a card very similar to this when printing the members of a
partitioned card image file. But there we wanted to print all 80 columns, and
here we just want to duplicate the first 72 columns of our card deck, reserving
columns 73–80 for our new sequence numbers.

The first control card will also look somewhat familiar. Its action word is
PUNCH, and it has three parameters. The first, as you might have guessed, is
MAXFLDS=1, to indicate that a RECORD control card follows. But the other
two parameters are new and are used to assign the sequence numbers:

CDSEQ. This specifies the sequence number you want put on the first card.
(CDSEQ stands for *Card Sequ*ence number). If you want to start with 0 on
the first card, you say:

```
CDSEQ=0
```

CDINCR. This tells by how much you want the sequence numbers on the
rest of the cards to be incremented. If you say

```
CDINCR=100
```

then the second card will have a sequence number of 100, the third will
have 200, and so on, each being 100 higher than the previous card.

So the whole control card is:

```
PUNCH   MAXFLDS=1,CDSEQ=0,CDINCR=100
```

And both control cards together look like this:

```
PUNCH       MAXFLDS=1,CDSEQ=0,CDINCR=100
RECORD    FIELD=(72)
```

And the whole job:

```
//SEQCARDS      JOB      (accnt),NAME,MSGLEVEL=(1,1)
//STEP1         EXEC     PGM=IEBPTPCH
//SYSPRINT      DD       SYSOUT=A
//SYSUT1        DD       *

              [card deck to be resequenced goes here]

/*
//SYSUT2        DD       SYSOUT=B
//SYSIN         DD
    PUNCH       MAXFLDS=1,CDSEQ=0,CDINCR=100
    RECORD    FIELD=(72)
/*
//
```

Rule 34. To duplicate a card deck and put new sequence numbers in columns 73–80 of the new card deck using IEBPTPCH requires two DD cards. SYSUT1 is the name of the first, which refers to the old card deck (SYSUT1 DD *) and is followed by the deck itself; the name of the second DD card is SYSUT2, which refers to the card punch (SYSOUT=B). There are two control cards. PUNCH is the action word of the first, and its three parameters are: MAXFLDS=1; CDSEQ, to assign a beginning sequence number; and CDINCR, to assign an increment for following sequence numbers. The second control card is RECORD FIELD=(72), meaning you just want to duplicate the first 72 columns of the old card deck.

QUESTIONS

1. What do the letters PTPCH stand for in IEBPTPCH?
2. IEBPTPCH requires two DD cards besides those for SYSPRINT and SYSIN; what do their names have to be?
3. *a.* Give the whole SYSUT2 DD card if we are printing.
   b. If we are punching.

4. Give the whole SYSUT1 DD card if we are printing from the following:
    a. A file called FILE on disk D10010 (not cataloged).
    b. A file called FILE2 on disk D10010 (cataloged).
5. When being used to print members of a card image file, what are the three action words of the three possible control cards?
6. What is the parameter on the following:
    a. MEMBER card.
    b. RECORD card.
7. What does the whole RECORD card always look like when printing partitioned card image files?
8. Which parameter on the PRINT or PUNCH control card is used to specify the following:
    a. How many MEMBER cards follow.
    b. How many RECORD cards follow.
9. If you have both MEMBER and RECORD cards, they must come in pairs for each member. Which of the two cards must precede the other?
10. Give the pair of MEMBER and RECORD cards that refer to a card image member called MEMA.
11. What parameter on the PRINT control card indicates that the file is partitioned?
12. Give all the control cards needed to print the member MEMB of a partitioned card image file.
13. Which of the three control cards can be left out when printing or punching all the members of a partitioned card image file?
14. If so, which parameters on the PRINT control card can then also be left out?
15. Give the control cards needed to print out all the members of a partitioned card image file.
16. *a.* Which of the three control cards changes if you want to punch out a member instead of printing it?
    b. What changes on it?
    c. Do any of its parameters change?
17. If you are punching out a member, what is the parameter on the SYSUT2 DD card?
18. When duplicating a card deck using IEBPTPCH, in which columns can you also put new sequence numbers?
19. If you just want to duplicate all 80 columns of a card deck, which other Utility will also do that for you?
20. Say that you want to use IEBPTPCH to duplicate a card deck.
    a. What does the SYSUT1 DD card have as its one parameter?
    b. What immediately follows the SYSUT1 DD card?
    c. What does the SYSUT2 DD card have as its one parameter?

21. *a.* When duplicating a card deck and adding sequence numbers in columns 73–80, what are the action words of the two control cards needed?
    b. Give the whole RECORD control card.
    c. How does the RECORD control card differ from that used when printing a card image file?
22. What parameter is necessary on the PUNCH control card to indicate that a RECORD control card follows?
23. What two parameters on the PUNCH control card specify what the sequence numbers will be?
24. *a.* If we want to have the first sequence number be 0 and the rest incremented by 10, what would these two parameters be?
    b. What would the two control cards be in this case?

11 IEBUPDTE

Imagine that out on a disk there is a partitioned file with a group of members, and each member contains a number of card images. We've already seen how IEBPTPCH can print out those members so you can see what they look like. IEBUPDTE can update members already there.

Instead of going through all the possible things IEBUPDTE can do, it might be best to become familiar with it by using a specific example. Let's say that the partitioned card image file we're working with is SYS1.PROCLIB, that it is cataloged, and that we want to add to it a member with JCL that looks like this:

```
//STEP1       EXEC   PGM=EXAMPLE
//SYSPRINT   DD      SYSOUT=A
```

This JCL itself is just an example—it has no meaning—but we should still be able to use IEBUPDTE to make these two card images a new member of SYS1.PROCLIB, and then update this new member once it's there.

The DD Cards

Updating a file means changing the information already in the file. This involves reading the original information and then writing it back "updated." There are two DD cards needed for this: the first, which must have the name SYSUT1, describes the file being read from; the second, which must have the name SYSUT2, describes the file being written to. But since updating means reading and writing to the same file, both DD cards refer to the same file, the one being updated.

A file being updated has to be an old file on disk. The JCL rules tell us that this is file type number 1, if uncataloged (DSN, UNIT, VOL, DISP) or file type number 2, if cataloged (DSN, DISP). In our example, we use SYS1.PROCLIB, which is cataloged, so the two DD cards are:

```
//SYSUT1   DD   DSNAME=SYS1.PROCLIB,DISP=OLD
//SYSUT2   DD   DSNAME=SYS1.PROCLIB,DISP=OLD
```

Note here that we say DISP=OLD, which locks out other programs from using SYS1.PROCLIB until we are done. This is necessary because we're changing the contents of the file, and we don't want anyone else to use it until it becomes stable again after our job is done.

1. Add a member to a partitioned card image file

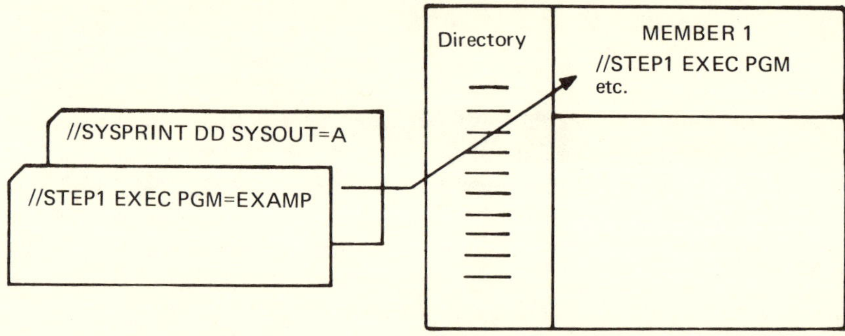

2. Change the contents of a partitioned card image file

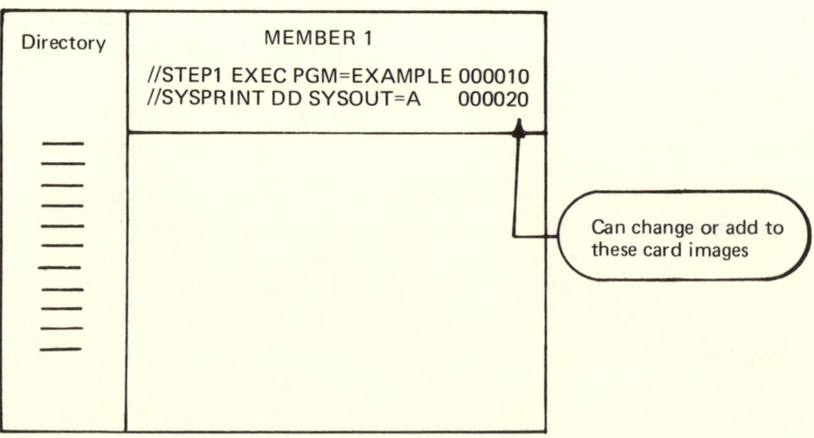

Fig. 11.1.   IEBUPDTE can add to or change the contents of a partitioned card image file.

Rule 35. Modifying a partitioned card image file using IEBUPDTE requires
two DD cards, the first with the name SYSUT1, and the second with
the name SYSUT2. They both refer to the same file, the one being
updated, which is an old file on disk.

The Control Cards

There are five kinds of control cards used in various arrangements. First,
we'll describe what they are, and later we'll see how they're used. Unlike the
control cards for any other Utility, these control cards must have a ./ in columns 1 and 2. After the ./ comes at least one blank, then the action word,
then at least one more blank, followed by the parameters.

1. The ADD card is used whenever you want to add a new member to a partitioned file. Its action word is ADD, and it has two parameters:

NAME. This specifies the name you want to give to the new member you
are adding. NAME=SAMPLE assigns the name SAMPLE to the new member.

LIST=ALL. This asks that a new member be printed out for you to look at.
Here is an example of the ADD card:

```
./  ADD   NAME=SAMPLE,LIST=ALL
```

It means "Add a new member to the file, give it the name SAMPLE, and print
it out for me to look at."

2. The NUMBER card always follows the ADD card, and puts in columns
73–80 numbers of the card images that make up the member you are adding.
From then on, each card image can be referred to by its number in columns
73–80. The NUMBER card has NUMBER as its action word and has two parameters:

NEW1. This specifies the number that the first card image is to have in
columns 73–80. NEW1=10 means that the first card will have the number
00000010 in columns 73–80.

INCR. Here you specify how much larger you want the number in each
card to be than the number in the card before it (the increment). If you
say INCR=10 (along with NEW1=10), then the second card will have the
number 00000020 in columns 73–80, the third card will have the number 00000030, and so on.

An example of the NUMBER card is

```
./  NUMBER   NEW1=10,INCR=10
```

It means: Number the card images of the new member being added, give the
first card the number 00000010 in columns 73–80, and add 10 to the number
in each card after that.

3. The CHANGE card. Let's say you already have a member out there in a

partitioned file, and you want to change what some of its card images look like. This card specifies what changes you want to make. Its action word is CHANGE, and it has two parameters:

NAME. This specifies the name of the member you want to change. NAME= SAMPLE means you want to make some changes to the card images in the member SAMPLE.

UPDATE=INPLACE. This specifies that the member can stay in the room it already has, for the change involves only new card images being laid right over old ones. You can't say this if card images are being added or inserted, for then the member will have to move to a larger room and can't be updated in the same place.

The card used to replace information in the member SAMPLE would be:

    ./   CHANGE   NAME=SAMPLE,UPDATE=INPLACE

But the card used to add or insert new information to the member SAMPLE would be just:

    ./   CHANGE   NAME=SAMPLE

4. The DELETE card is used in cases where we find that some of the card images in a member are no longer needed. We get rid of them with the DELETE card, identifying which card images are to be deleted with two parameters:

SEQ1. Here we give the sequence number (in columns 73–80) of the first card image to be deleted.

SEQ2. Here we give the sequence number of the last card image to be deleted.

For example, if we say,

    ./   DELETE   SEQ1=30,SEQ2=60

then all the card images with sequence numbers between and including 00000030 and 00000060 will be deleted.

If just one card image is to be gotten rid of, both SEQ1 and SEQ2 refer to its sequence number. The following card gets rid of the one card image with the sequence number of 00000030:

    ./   DELETE   SEQ1=30,SEQ2=30

5. The ENDUP card is a simple card that is always the last control card. It has no parameters and looks like this:

    ./   ENDUP

Here is a table of the five control cards and their parameters:

```
./  ADD        NAME=LIST,ALL
./  NUMBER     NEW1=,INCR=
./  CHANGE     NAME=,UPDATE=INPLACE
./  DELETE     SEQ2=,SEQ2=
./  ENDUP
```

Now we'll describe what they can do and how to use them.

ADDING A CARD IMAGE MEMBER

Adding a new member uses three control cards—ADD, NUMBER, and
ENDUP. First comes the ADD card, giving the new member a name, and then
the NUMBER card, assigning numbers to the card images in columns 73–80.
Immediately after that come the actual cards that will become the new member. Then, at the very end, is the ENDUP card. For our example, we want to
add a member with these two card images:

```
//STEP1      EXEC  PGM=EXAMPLE
//SYSPRINT   DD    SYSOUT=A
```

So the control card information should be:

```
./  ADD        NAME=SAMPLE,LIST=ALL
./  NUMBER     NEW1=10,INCR=10
//STEP1        EXEC  PGM=EXAMPLE
//SYSPRINT     DD    SYSOUT=A
./  ENDUP
```

This adds a new member named SAMPLE to the partitioned file, which, with
its numbers in columns 73–80, will look like this:

```
//STEP1      EXEC  PGM=EXAMPLE                    00000010
//SYSPRINT   DD    SYSOUT=A                       00000020
```

Rule 36. Adding a new member to a partitioned card image file using
         IEBUPDTE requires three control cards, each with a ./ in columns
         1 and 2. ADD is the action word on the first. Its two parameters are:
         NAME, giving a name to the new member; and LIST=ALL, saying you
         want the member printed out. NUMBER is the action word on the
         second control card. Its parameters are: NEW1, specifying the number
         the first card image is to have in columns 73–80; and INCR, saying
         how much larger than the one before it you want the number of
         each card image to be. ENDUP is the action word of the last card; it

has no parameters. Between the NUMBER and ENDUP cards are put the actual cards that are to become the new member.

The whole job:

```
//ADDMEM            JOB       (accnt),NAME,MSGLEVEL=(1,1)
//STEP1             EXEC      PGM=IEBUPDTE
//SYSPRINT          DD        SYSOUT=A
//SYSUT1            DD        DSN=SYS1.PROCLIB,DISP=OLD
//SYSUT2            DD        DSN=SYS1.PROCLIB,DISP=OLD
//SYSIN             DD        DATA
./   ADD       NAME=SAMPLE,LIST=ALL
./   NUMBER    NEW1=10,INCR=10
//STEP1             EXEC      PGM=EXAMPLE
//SYSPRINT          DD        SYSOUT=A
./   ENDUP
/*
//
```

You may notice that the SYSIN DD card is slightly different from usual, having the word DATA where the * usually goes. This says that there may be JCL cards in the information that follows, and to treat them as ordinary information and not as JCL cards. It knows to start treating JCL cards as such after it comes to a /* card. Let's make this a separate rule.

Rule 37. When using IEBUPDTE, the SYSIN DD card should look like this—

```
//SYSIN  DD  DATA
```

—telling the system not to treat any JCL cards that follow as JCL cards until after the next /* card.

Note: If the cards that you want to become the new member already have sequence numbers in columns 73–80, then the NUMBER control card can be left out.

CHANGING A MEMBER OF A PARTITIONED CARD IMAGE FILE

Now that we've added our member, it looks like this:

```
//STEP1      EXEC   PGM=EXAMPLE                         00000010
//SYSPRINT   DD     SYSOUT=A                            00000020
```

To change this member, you use the numbers in columns 73–80 to identify the cards that you want to replace or between which you want to insert new cards. A new card with the number 00000010 in columns 73–80 will replace

the old card with that number. With the number 00000015, it will, in our example, be inserted between the two cards already there. This is how it's done:
the CHANGE control card comes first, and the ENDUP card goes last. In between the two control cards you put the new card to be used to update the
member, with the number in columns 73–80 that tells where it should be put.
To change our member SAMPLE by replacing the EXEC card with this new
card:

```
//STEP2  EXEC  PGM=EXAMPLE2
```

This will do it:

```
./  CHANGE   NAME=SAMPLE,UPDATE=INPLACE
//STEP2  EXEC  PGM=EXAMPLE2                                    00000010
./  ENDUP
```

The whole thing is that number in columns 73–80, which tells it where to replace the card that has the number 00000010; UPDATE=INPLACE is used because the change involves only a replacement and no additions.

Rule 38. Replacing card images of a member in a partitioned card image file
using IEBUPDTE requires two control cards, both with a ./ in columns 1 and 2. CHANGE is the action word on the first. Its two parameters are NAME, giving the name of the member to be updated;
and UPDATE=INPLACE, saying that the member can remain in the
room it now occupies. ENDUP is the action word of the second control card, which has no parameters. In between them are put the replacement cards, each having in columns 73–80 the number that
matches the card image it is to replace.

The whole job:

```
//UPDATE1           JOB     (accnt),NAME,MSGLEVEL=(1,1)
//STEP1             EXEC    PGM=IEBUPDTE
//SYSPRINT          DD      SYSOUT=A
//SYSUT1            DD      DSN=SYS1.PROCLIB,DISP=OLD
//SYSUT2            DD      DSN=SYS1.PROCLIB,DISP=OLD
//SYSIN             DD      DATA
./    CHANGE  NAME=SAMPLE,UPDATE=INPLACE
//STEP2             EXEC  PGM=EXAMPLE2                     00000010
./    ENDUP
/*
//
```

Note: The SYSIN DD card again says DATA, so that the JCL card sand-
wiched in between the two control cards is not mistaken for an actual JCL
card.

Now our member looks like this:

```
//STEP2        EXEC   PGM=EXAMPLE2                          00000010
//SYSPRINT   DD      SYSOUT=A                               00000020
```

Inserting

Let's say we want to insert a new card image in between the two that are already there, one that looks like this:

```
//EXTRADD   DD   SYSOUT=A
```

The number in columns 73–80 again will tell where to put it, so to indicate an insertion means giving the new card a number between 10 and 20—for instance, 15. As before, the CHANGE card comes first, naming the member to be updated, but this time UPDATE=INPLACE is left out, because the change will make the member larger. The ENDUP card comes last, and in between goes the insertion card with the number 00000015 in columns 73–80.

```
./  CHANGE   NAME=SAMPLE
//EXTRADD   DD                    SYSOUT=A                  00000015
./  ENDUP
```

After the change, the member would look like this:

```
//STEP2        EXEC   PGM=EXAMPLE2                          00000010
//EXTRADD    DD      SYSOUT=A                               00000015
//SYSPRINT   DD      SYSOUT=A                               00000020
```

Rule 39. Adding new card images to a member of a partitioned card image file using IEBUPDTE requires two control cards, both with a ./ in columns 1 and 2. CHANGE is the action word of the first. Its one parameter is NAME, giving the name of the member to be changed. ENDUP is the action word of the second control card, and it has no parameters. In between them are put the cards to be added, each having in columns 73–80 a number that indicates in between which card images it should be inserted.

The whole job is:

```
//UPDATE2        JOB      (accnt),NAME,MSGLEVEL=(1,1)
//STEP1          EXEC     PGM=IEBUPDTE
//SYSPRINT       DD       SYSOUT=A
//SYSUT1         DD       DSN=SYS1.PROCLIB,DISP=OLD
//SYSUT2         DD       DSN=SYS1.PROCLIB,DISP=OLD
//SYSIN          DD       DATA
./  CHANGE   NAME=SAMPLE
```

```
//EXTRADD            DD      SYSOUT=A            00000015
./  ENDUP
/*
//
```

Deleting

Now suppose we decide that we don't want some of the card images in our member anymore. Let's say, for example, that even though our sample member at this point has only three card images, we want to get rid of the last two card images, those with the sequence numbers 15 and 20.

First, we need the CHANGE control card, naming the member to be changed:

```
./  CHANGE   NAME=SAMPLE
```

Next, we have a DELETE control card, specifying the numbers 15 and 20.

```
./  DELETE   SEQ1=15,SEQ2=20
```

It's as simple as that. The ENDUP control card is not needed here. Both cards together would look like this:

```
./  CHANGE   NAME=SAMPLE
./  DELETE   SEQ1=15,SEQ2=20
```

If there were any card images with sequence numbers between 15 and 20, they would be deleted, too.

After the change, our decimated member would look like this:

```
//STEP2  EXEC  PGM=EXAMPLE2                       00000010
```

If, on the other hand, we had just wanted to delete one card— the one with sequence number of 15, for example—the SEQ1 and SEQ2 parameters would both have referred to that card, and the DELETE control card would have been:

```
./  DELETE   SEQ1=15,SEQ2=15
```

Both control cards together are:

```
./  CHANGE   NAME=SAMPLE
./  DELETE   SEQ1=15,SEQ2=15
```

Rule 40. Deleting card images from a member of a partitioned card image file
        using IEBUPDTE requires two cards, both with a ./ in columns 1
        and 2. CHANGE is the action word of the first. Its one parameter is
        NAME, giving the name of the member to be changed. DELETE is the

action word of the second control card, where SEQ1 gives the sequence number of the first card image to be deleted and SEQ2 gives the sequence number of the last card image to be deleted; the card images with those two sequence numbers and any in between are deleted. If only one card image is to be deleted, both SEQ1 and SEQ2 give the sequence number of the same card image, the one to be deleted.

The whole job:

```
//DELETE      JOB      (accnt),NAME,MSGLEVEL=(1,1)
//STEP1       EXEC     PGM=IEBUPDTE
//SYSPRINT    DD       SYSOUT=A
//SYSUT1      DD       DSN=SYS1.PROCLIB,DISP=OLD
//SYSUT2      DD       DSN=SYS1.PROCLIB,DISP=OLD
//SYSIN       DD       *
./CHANGE    NAME=SAMPLE
./DELETE    SEQ1=15,SEQ2=20
/*
//
```

CREATING A NEW PARTITIONED CARD IMAGE FILE

So far, we have discussed the many ways of modifying an existing partitioned card image file: adding members and changing members. Now, last, we will describe how to create a new partitioned card image file.

The DD Card

The process is very similar to adding a member to an existing file. The difference is that only the SYSUT2 DD card is needed, and it will describe a new file on disk, which is file type number 5, with the DSN, UNIT, DISP=(NEW, KEEP), and SPACE parameters. The VOL=SER parameter will be used, too, if you want to put it on a specific disk pack, which would probably be the case.

Let's say that we want the new file to be named NEWFILE, that we want to give it 50 tracks of disk space on disk D10040, and that we think there never will be more than 100 members in it. Our DD card would look like this:

```
//SYSUT2  DD  DSN=NEWFILE,UNIT=3330,VOL=SER=D10040,
//               DISP=(NEW,KEEP),SPACE=(TRK,(50,,34))
```

Remember that odd-looking SPACE parameter? That number 34 after the two commas reserves space for the directory when creating a partitioned file; it should be equal to about one-third of the anticipated number of members (one third of 100 is about 34). The SYSUT1 DD card is left out entirely.

The Control Cards

The control cards are just like those for adding a member to an existing card image file. For example, if we wanted to put into our partitioned file a member called SAMPLE, which looked like this—

```
//STEP1       EXEC  PGM=EXAMPLE
//SYSPRINT    DD    SYSOUT=A
```

—the control card would be exactly the same as when adding to an existing file:

```
./  ADD       NAME=SAMPLE,LIST=ALL
./  NUMBER  NEW1=10,INCR=10
//STEP1       EXEC  PGM=EXAMPLE
//SYSPRINT    DD    SYSOUT=A
./  ENDUP
```

But let's say we want to add two members to our new partitioned card image file, not just one, and we want the second member to be named SAMPLE2 and to look like this:

```
//STEP2       EXEC  PGM=EXAMPLE2
//SYSPRINT    DD    SYSOUT=A
```

Then our control cards look like this:

```
./  ADD       NAME=SAMPLE,LIST=ALL
./  NUMBER  NEW1=10,INCR=10
//STEP1       EXEC   PGM=EXAMPLE
//SYSPRINT    DD     SYSOUT=A
./  ADD       NAME=SAMPLE2,LIST=ALL
./  NUMBER  NEW1=10,INCR=10
//STEP2       EXEC   PGM=EXAMPLE2
//SYSPRINT    DD     SYSOUT=A
./  ENDUP
```

In short, we just have a new pair of ADD and NUMBER control cards followed by each new member, with the ADD control cards giving each member a different name. There's only one ENDUP card, and that goes at the very end.
Rule 41. When creating a new partitioned card image file using IEBUPDTE, the SYSUT1 DD card is left out; the SYSUT2 DD card is for a new

file on disk (DSN, UNIT, DISP=(NEW,KEEP), SPACE (reserving space
for the directory, too), and usually VOL=SER to put it on a specific
pack). The control cards are the same as for adding to an existing
partitioned card image file, with the ADD and NUMBER control cards
being repeated for and followed by each new member. The ADD
control card gives each member a different name, and there is only
one ENDUP card, which goes at the very end.

The whole job:

```
//NEWPDS      JOB     (accnt),NAME,MSGLEVEL=(1,1)
//STEP1       EXEC    PGM=IEBUPDTE
//SYSPRINT    DD      SYSOUT=A
//SYSUT2      DD      DSN=NEWFILE,UNIT=3330,VOL=SER=D10040,
//                    SPACE=(TRK,(50,,34))
//SYSIN       DD      DATA
./  ADD       NAME=SAMPLE,LIST=ALL
./  NUMBER    NEW1=10,INCR=10
//STEP1       EXEC    PGM=EXAMPLE
//SYSPRINT    DD      SYSOUT=A
./  ADD       NAME=SAMPLE2,LIST=ALL
./  NUMBER    NEW1=10,INCR=10
//STEP2       EXEC    PGM=EXAMPLE2
//SYSPRINT    DD      SYSOUT=A
./  ENDUP
/*
//
```

QUESTIONS

1. Which of the following must be true about a file with which IEBUPDTE
   works?
   a. It must be sequential.
   b. It must be partitioned.
   c. It must contain card images.
   d. It must contain translated programs.
2. When modifying an existing partitioned file, IEBUPDTE needs two DD cards.
   a. What must their DD names be?
   b. How many files are referred to by these two DD cards.
3. What is the DISP parameter on each of these two DD cards.
4. *a.* What other parameters, besides the DISP parameter, are needed on
   these two DD cards if the file is not cataloged?
   b. What are needed if the file is cataloged?

5. What is the only difference between the two DD cards?
6. *a.* What must be in columns 1 and 2 of every IEBUPDTE control card?
   b. Is IEBUPDTE the only Utility that requires this?
7. What are the action words on the five types of control cards for IEBUPDTE?
8. Can the ADD and CHANGE control cards be found in the same operation?
9. *a.* Which of the five types of control cards is always last?
   b. What are its parameters?
10. When adding a member to a partitioned card image file, what three control cards are needed?
11. What is the function of the NUMBER control card?
12. If you have an ADD and a NUMBER control card together, which must come first?
13. What parameter on the ADD control card gives the new member its name?
14. How do we specify that we want the member to be printed for us to look at?
15. Which control card indicates that we want to put a whole new member into the partitioned file?
16. *a.* What are the two parameters on the NUMBER control card?
    b. What would they be if we wanted the first sequence number to be 100 and the rest to be incremented by 100?
17. What would happen if we left out the NUMBER control card?
18. Give the three control cards necessary to add a member called NEWMEM, having IEBUPDTE put sequence numbers in columns 73–80, beginning with 100 and incrementing the rest by 100.
19. Between which two control cards would the cards of the new member be put?
20. Can the cards that are becoming the new member include actual JCL cards?
21. If JCL cards are included, what must the SYSIN DD card look like?
22. What special JCL card indicates that JCL cards can be treated like real JCL cards again, instead of data cards becoming a new member?
23. What would happen to the real JCL cards that follow your job if this special JCL card is left out?
24. What action word indicates that a member is to have card images added or replaced?
25. What parameter on this control card indicates *which* member is to be changed?
26. What must be in columns 73–80 of the member's card images if the member is to be changed?
27. What must be in columns 73–80 of the cards that are meant to be additions or replacements to the member?

28. What parameter on the CHANGE control card indicates that card images will only be replaced, that there will be no additions, and that the member will remain the same size?
29. If additions are to be made, what parameters are needed on the CHANGE control card?
30. Give the two control cards needed in the following instances:
    a. If we want simply to replace a card in a member called MEM.
    b. If we want to add a card to the member called MEM.
31. Between what two control cards do the additions and/or replacements go?
32. What two control cards are needed to get rid of specific card images?
33. What is named on the first control card?
34. What are the two parameters on the DELETE control card?
35. What would these two parameters look like if we wanted to do the following:
    a. Get rid of all card images with sequence numbers between and including 500 and 900.
    b. Delete just one card image with the sequence number 30.
36. When deleting card images, is the ENDUP control card needed?
37. Give the control cards needed to delete the card images in the member MEM1, with the sequence numbers between and including 350 and 450.
38. When creating a partitioned card image file using IEBUPDTE, which of the two DD cards usually required for IEBUPDTE is not needed?
39. What is the DDname of the DD card that is needed?
40. What kind of file does this DD card describe? (Select one.)
    a. A new file on tape.
    b. A new file on disk.
    c. An old file on disk.
41. What is its DISP parameter?
42. Give its SPACE parameter if we want to give it 105 tracks of disk space, and we anticipate its having no more than 150 members.
43. For each member to be put into the partitioned file, what two control cards are needed?
44. Which of these control cards assigns each member a different name?
45. *a.* If I am putting ten members in my partitioned file, how many pairs of ADD and NUMBER control cards will I need?
    b. How many ENDUP control cards will there be?
    c. Where is the ENDUP control card placed?

12 HAVING UTILITIES DO MORE THAN ONE THING AT A TIME

You should now be familiar with our eight Utilities and be able to make them do what you want. As you see, they can perform a great many valuable and necessary functions. I hope the logic behind the many rules was made as clear as possible.

For simplicity's sake, we separated each function of each Utility into a separate job. But most of the Utilities allow you to do more than one thing at a time. With IEHLIST, IEHDASDR, IEBCOPY, IEHMOVE, and IEHPROGM, you can add as many DD cards and control cards as you like, having them perform many functions on many files in the same job. For example, you can list several VTOCs or catalog several files at once. However, even though IEHDASDR will accept any number of control cards, it will not do more than six analyzes, dumps, or restores at the same time.

IEBPTPCH and IEBUPDTE are slightly more limited in that they can work only with their SYSUT1 and SYSUT2 files, but you can have as many control cards as you like. IEBGENER is the loner. It can do only one thing at a time, copying this to that.

QUESTIONS

(For the following questions, "in the same job" means the same as "in the same step.")

1. *a.* Can you list both the primary catalog and a secondary catalog in the same job?
   b. If the primary catalog is on disk D10040 and a secondary catalog is on D10020, give the DD cards and control cards required to list them (besides the SYSPRINT and SYSIN DD cards).
2. *a.* Can you compress three different partitioned files in the same job?

     b. If the DD names of the DD cards for the three files were FILE1, FILE2, and FILE3, give the control cards.

3. *a.* Is it possible to initialize three new disk packs at the same time?
   b. Can one create backup tapes for six disk packs at the same time?
   c. What would happen if you had control cards saying you wanted to create backup tapes for seven disk packs at the same time?

4. Can you catalog two files, rename four files, and scratch ten files in the same job?

5. *a.* Give the control cards needed to uncatalog the following four files: FILE, DISKFILE, TAPEFILE, LIBFILE.
   b. How many DD cards would be required?
   c. Why?

6. Can you catalog a file and list the catalog in the same job?

7. *a.* If we wanted to scratch files off ten different disk packs, how many DD cards would be required to describe them?
   b. If we wanted to scratch ten files off the same disk pack, how many DD cards would be required?

8. *a.* Can we copy selected members from five different partitioned files all to one other partitioned file?
   b. How many DD cards would be required to describe those files?

9. *a.* Can we print out card image members from two different partitioned files in the same job?
   b. Why?

10. *a.* Can we update the members of three partitioned card image files in the same job?
   b. Why?
   c. Can we update ten different members of the same partitioned card image file in the same job?
   d. Give the control cards needed to add a card image to two different members named MEM1 and MEM2, both in the same partitioned card image file.

11. What is common among the DDname requirements for the files you are working with when using IEBPTPCH, IEBUPDTE, and IEBGENER?

12. *a.* Can we put a card file to a tape and duplicate another card deck in the same job?
   b. How could we do both at the same time?

SUMMARY

Here, for review and reference, is the chart of action words and parameters and a list of all the rules that we've assembled as we've gone along.

ACTION WORDS AND PARAMETERS

IEHLIST	LISTVTOC	FORMAT,VOL=
	LISTPDS	➡ DSNAME=,VOL=
	LISTCTLG	CVOL=
	ANALYZE	➡ TODD=,VTOC=,EXTENT=,NEWVOLID=, PURGE=YES,PASSES=
IEHDASDR	DUMP	FROMDD=,TODD=,BEGIN=,END=
	RESTORE	➡ FROMDD=,TODD=,PURGE=YES
	LABEL	TODD=,NEWVOLID=
IEBCOPY	COPY	INDD=,OUTDD=
	SELECT	➡ MEMBER=
	EXCLUDE	MEMBER=
IEHMOVE	COPY	➡ PDS=,FROM=,FROMDD=,TO=,TODD=
IEHPROGM	CATLG	DSNAME=,VOL=
	UNCATLG	DSNAME=
	SCRATCH	➡ DSNAME=,VOL=,PURGE,VTOC,MEMBER=
	RENAME	DSNAME=,VOL=,MEMBER=,NEWNAME=
IEBPTPCH	PRINT	TYPORG=PO,MAXNAME=,MAXFLDS=
	MEMBER	NAME=
	RECORD	➡ FIELD=
	PUNCH	TYPORG=PO,MAXNAME=,MAXFLDS=, CDSEQ=,CDINCR=

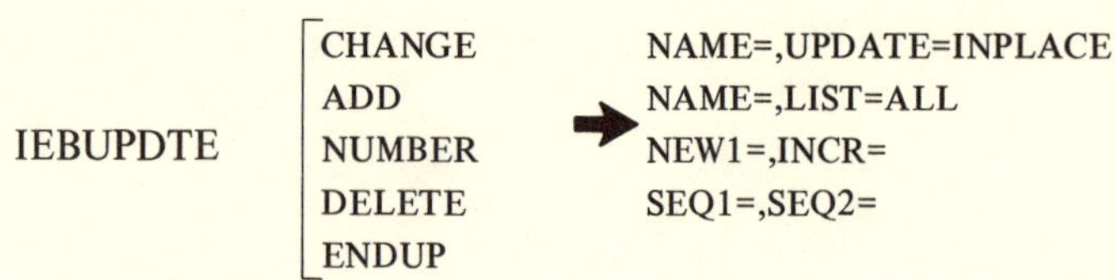

IEBUPDTE
- CHANGE   NAME=,UPDATE=INPLACE
- ADD   NAME=,LIST=ALL
- NUMBER   NEW1=,INCR=
- DELETE   SEQ1=,SEQ2=
- ENDUP

THE 41 RULES, WITH EXAMPLES

IEHLIST

1. IEHLIST needs one DD card for the disk pack you want information from, specifying the whole pack, with any DD name.

   ```
   //DISK   DD   UNIT=3330,VOL=SER=D10040,DISP=OLD
   ```

2. Printing a VTOC using IEHLIST requires one control card, and LISTVTOC is the action word. The parameters are: FORMAT, which stands alone; and VOL, which gives the unit type and number of the pack whose VTOC is being listed.

   ```
   //LISTVTOC   JOB     (accnt),NAME,MSGLEVEL=(1,1)
   //STEP1      EXEC   PGM=IEHLIST
   //SYSPRINT   DD       SYSOUT=A
   //DISK       DD       UNIT=3330,VOL=SER=D10040,DISP=OLD
   //SYSIN      DD       *
        LISTVTOC   FORMAT,VOL=3330=D10040
   /*
   //
   ```

3. Listing the directory of a partitioned file using IEHLIST requires one control card, and LISTPDS is the action word. The parameters are: DSNAME, to name the file; and VOL, to give the unit type and pack number the file is on.

   ```
   //LISTLIB    JOB     (accnt),NAME,MSGLEVEL=(1,1)
   //STEP1      EXEC   PGM=IEHLIST
   //SYSPRINT   DD       SYSOUT=A
   //DISK       DD       UNIT=3330,VOL=SER=D10040,DISP=OLD
   //SYSIN      DD       *
        LISTPDS   DSNAME=LOADLIB,VOL=3330=D10040
   /*
   //
   ```

4. Listing the catalog using IEHLIST requires one control card, and LISTCTLG
   is the action word. There are no other parameters.

```
//LISTCAT      JOB      (accnt),NAME,MSGLEVEL=(1,1)
//STEP1        EXEC     PGM=IEHLIST
//SYSPRINT     DD       SYSOUT=A
//DRUM         DD       UNIT=2305,VOL=SER=DD2305,DISP=OLD
//SYSIN        DD       *
        LISTCTLG
/*
//
```

5. Listing a secondary catalog using IEHLIST requires one control card, and
   LISTCTLG is the action word. The one parameter is CVOL, where you give
   the unit type and serial number of the disk pack or drum that the secondary catalog is on.

```
/SECCATLG     JOB      (accnt),NAME,MSGLEVEL=(1,1)
//STEP1        EXEC     PGM=IEHLIST
//SYSPRINT     DD       SYSOUT=A
//DISK         DD       UNIT=3330,VOL=SER=D10040,DISP=OLD
//SYSIN        DD       *
        LISTCTLG   CVOL=3330=D10040
/*
//
```

IEHDASDR

6. Initializing a new disk pack using IEHDASDR requires no DD card, and
   the disk must be offline. ANALYZE is the action word. The parameters
   are: TODD, to specify the offline disk drive; VTOC, which tells where the
   VTOC is to begin; EXTENT, which gives the length of the VTOC; and
   NEWVOLID, which assigns a volume serial number.

```
//INITLIZE     JOB      (accnt),NAME,MSGLEVEL=(1,1)
//STEP1        EXEC     PGM=IEHDASDR
//SYSPRINT     DD       SYSOUT=A
//SYSIN        DD       *
        ANALYZE   TODD=230,VTOC=1,EXTENT=5,NEWVOLID=D10040
/*
//
```

7. Reinitializing a disk pack using IEHDASDR, the disk is left online, and
   one DD card with any DDname is needed for the whole pack. ANALYZE
   is the action word. The parameters VTOC, EXTENT, and NEWVOLID are
   the same as for the offline initialization, TODD names the DD card, and
   PURGE=YES allows it to erase information on the pack.

```
//ANALYZE    JOB     (accnt),NAME,MSGLEVEL=(1,1)
//STEP1       EXEC  PGM=IEHDASDR
//SYSPRINT   DD      SYSOUT=A
//DISK        DD      UNIT=3330,VOL=SER=D10040,DISP=OLD
//SYSIN       DD      *
     ANALYZE   TODD=DISK,VTOC=1,EXTENT=5,NEWVOLID=D10040, C
               PURGE=YES
/*
//
```

8. Giving an old pack a new volume serial number by using IEHDASDR is
   called relabeling a disk pack. It has one DD card, referring to the whole
   pack being relabeled. The action word on the control card is LABEL, and
   the two parameters are TODD, naming the DD card, and NEWVOLID, giving the new volume serial number.

```
//RELABEL    JOB     (accnt),NAME,MSGLEVEL=(1,1)
//STEP1       EXEC  PGM=IEHDASDR
//SYSPRINT   DD      SYSOUT=A
//DISK        DD      UNIT=3330,VOL=SER=D10040,DISP=OLD
//SYSIN       DD      *
     LABEL   TODD=DISK,NEWVOLID=D10041
/*
//
```

9. Creating a backup tape using IEHDASDR requires two DD cards, one for
   the disk you're dumping from (specifying the whole pack), and the other
   for the tape you're dumping to (specifying a new tape). On the control
   card, DUMP is the action word. The parameters are: FROMDD, giving the
   name of the disk DD card; and TODD, giving the name of the tape DD
   card.

```
//DUMP       JOB     (accnt),NAME,MSGLEVEL=(1,1)
//STEP1       EXEC  PGM=IEHDASDR
//SYSPRINT   DD      SYSOUT=A
//DISK        DD      UNIT=3330,VOL=SER=D10040,DISP=OLD
//TAPE        DD      DSN=TAPE,UNIT=3400-3,DISP=(NEW,KEEP)
//SYSIN       DD      *
     DUMP   FROMDD=DISK,TODD=TAPE
/*
//
```

10. Printing specific tracks of a disk pack using IEHDASDR is part of the
    dump function, and is the same as dumping the pack to tape except that
    the DD card for the tape is left out. The TODD parameter refers to the

SYSPRINT file (dumping to the printer), and the two new parameters are BEGIN and END, giving the cylinder and track numbers (eight hexadecimal numbers in all) with which to start and stop printing.

```
//PRINTRKS   JOB     (accnt),NAME,MSGLEVEL=(1,1)
//STEP1       EXEC    PGM=IEHDASDR
//SYSPRINT   DD      SYSOUT=A
//DISK       DD      UNIT=3330,VOL=SER=D10040,DISP=OLD
//SYSIN      DD      *
     DUMP   FROMDD=DISK,TODD=SYSPRINT,BEGIN=00050002,        C
            END=00060002
/*
//
```

11. Restoring a disk from a backup tape using IEHDASDR requires two DD cards: one is for the tape you are restoring from, specifying an old tape (DSNAME, VOL, UNIT, DISP=OLD); the other is for the disk you are restoring to, specifying the whole disk. On the control card, RESTORE is the action word. The parameters are: FROMDD, naming the DD card for the tape; TODD, naming the DD card for the disk; and PURGE=YES, allowing it to erase any information still on the disk.

```
//RESTORE    JOB     (accnt),NAME,MSGLEVEL=(1,1)
//STEP1       EXEC    PGM=IEHDASDR
//SYSPRINT   DD      SYSOUT=A
//TAPE       DD      DSN=TAPE,VOL=SER=004000,UNIT=3400-3,
//                   DISP=OLD
//DISK       DD      UNIT=3330,VOL=SER=D10040,DISP=OLD
//SYSIN      DD      *
     RESTORE   FROMDD=TAPE,TODD=DISK,PURGE=YES
/*
//
```

IEBGENER

12. IEBGENER requires a special parameter on its SYSUT2 (output) DD card—DCB=BLKSIZE=—where you specify how big you want to block the information on the output file. The blocksize must be an even multiple of the size of a record. For the card punch, it is always DCB=BLKSIZE=80 (unblocked); for the printer, it is always equal to the size of one record (also not blocked).

13. IEBGENER copies information from an input file to an output file. The name of the DD card for the input file must be SYSUT1, and can be cards (//SYSIN DD *) or an old file on tape or disk (DSN, UNIT, VOL=SER, DISP). The name of the DD card for the output file must be SYSUT2, which can

be the printer (SYSOUT=A), punched cards (SYSOUT=B), a new file on tape (DSN, UNIT, DISP), or a new file on disk (DSN, UNIT, VOL=SER, DISP, SPACE). The DCB=BLKSIZE parameter must also be on this card. No control card is needed, and its absence is indicated by a //SYSIN DD DUMMY card.

Copying tape to tape:

```
//DUPTAPE     JOB      (accnt),NAME,MSGLEVEL=(1,1)
//STEP1       EXEC     PGM=IEBGENER
//SYSPRINT    DD       SYSOUT-A
//SYSUT1      DD       DSN=TAPE,UNIT=3400-3,VOL=SER=004000,
//                     DISP=OLD
//SYSUT2      DD       DSN=TAPE,UNIT=3400-3,DISP=(NEW,KEEP),
//                     DCB=BLKSIZE=80
//SYSIN       DD       DUMMY
```

Tape to print:

```
//PRNTTAPE   JOB      (accnt),NAME,MSGLEVEL=(1,1)
//STEP1      DD       PGM=IEBGENER
//SYSPRINT   DD       SYSOUT=A
//SYSUT1     DD       DSN=TAPE,UNIT=3400-3,VOL=SER=004000,
//                    DISP=OLD
//SYSUT2     DD       SYSOUT=A,DCB=BLKSIZE=80
//SYSIN      DD       DUMMY
```

Card to tape:

```
//CARDTAPE    JOB      (accnt),NAME,MSGLEVEL=(1,1)
//STEP1       EXEC     PGM=IEBGENER
//SYSPRINT    DD       SYSOUT=A
//SYSUT1      DD       *
```

[card file to be put on tape goes here]

```
/*
//SYSUT2      DD       DSN=TAPE,UNIT=3400-3,DISP=(NEW,KEEP),
//                     DCB=BLKSIZE=80
//SYSIN       DD       DUMMY
```

IEBCOPY

14. IEBCOPY always uses two temporary work files on disk, and a DD card is needed for each (UNIT and SPACE parameters needed only). The DDnames

must be SYSUT3 and SYSUT4; each usually needs about five tracks of
space.

```
//SYSUT3  DD   UNIT=3330,SPACE=(TRK,5)
//SYSUT4  DD   UNIT=3330,SPACE=(TRK,5)
```

15. Copying a partitioned file from one disk to another using IEBCOPY requires four DD cards, two for work files SYSUT3 and SYSUT4 plus one for
the old file you are copying from (DSNAME, UNIT, VOL=SER, DISP) and
one for the new file you are copying to (DSNAME, UNIT, VOL=SER, DISP,
SPACE), both with any DD names. There is one control card, and COPY
is the action word. The two parameters are: INDD, giving the name of the
DD card describing the old file; and OUTDD, giving the name of the DD
card describing the new file.

```
//COPY       JOB    (accnt),NAME,MSGLEVEL=(1,1)
//STEP1      EXEC   PGM=IEBCOPY
//SYSPRINT   DD     SYSOUT=A
//FROM       DD     DSN=FROMLIB,UNIT=3330,VOL=SER=D10040,
//                  DISP=OLD
//TO         DD     DSN=TOLIB,UNIT=3330,VOL=SER=D10080,
//                  DISP=(NEW,KEEP),SPACE=(TRK,(400,,50))
//SYSUT3     DD     UNIT=3330,SPACE=(TRK,5)
//SYSUT4     DD     UNIT=3330,SPACE=(TRK,5)
//SYSIN      DD     *
     COPY    INDD=FROM,OUTDD=TO
/*
//
```

16. Copying individual members from one partitioned file to another using
IEBCOPY requires four DD cards: two for the SYSUT3 and SYSUT4 work
files, plus one for the old file from which you are copying (DSN, UNIT,
VOL=SER, DISP) and one for the old file to which you are copying (DSN,
UNIT, VOL=SER, DISP), both with any DDnames. There are two control
cards. COPY is the action word of the first, with the parameters INDD
and OUTDD: the action word for the second is either SELECT or EXCLUDE,
with the parameter MEMBER giving the names of the members you either
want included or excluded from the copy operation.

```
//COPYMEM  JOB    (accnt),NAME,MSGLEVEL=(1,1)
//STEP1    EXEC   PGM=IEBCOPY
//SYSPRINT DD     SYSOUT=A
//FROM     DD     DSN=FROMLIB,UNIT=3330,VOL=SER=D10040,
```

```
//                      DISP=OLD
//TO          DD        DSN=TOLIB,UNIT=3330,VOL=SER=D10080,DISP=OLD
//SYSUT3      DD        UNIT=3330,SPACE=(TRK,5)
//SYSUT4      DD        UNIT=3330,SPACE=(TRK,5)
//SYSIN       DD        *
      COPY      INDD=FROM,OUTDD=TO
      SELECT    MEMBER=(PROGA,PROGB)
/*
//
```

17. Compressing a partitioned file using IEBCOPY requires one DD card—be-sides those for the SYSUT3 and SYSUT4 work files—for the file being com-pressed, which is an old file on disk (DSN, UNIT, VOL, DISP). The card can have any DDname, and there is one control card. COPY is the action word. The two parameters INDD and OUTDD both specify the same name of the DD card for the file being compressed.

```
//COMPRESS    JOB       (accnt),NAME,MSGLEVEL=(1,1)
//STEP1       EXEC      PGM=IEBCOPY,REGION=100K
//SYSPRINT    DD        SYSOUT=A
//LIB         DD        DSNAME=LIBFILE,UNIT=3330,VOL=SER=D10040,
//                      DISP=OLD
//SYSUT3      DD        UNIT=3330,SPACE=(TRK,5)
//SYSUT4      DD        UNIT=3330,SPACE=(TRK,5)
//SYSIN       DD        *
      COPY    INDD=LIB,OUTDD=LIB
/*
//
```

18. When compressing a partitioned file using IEBCOPY, add the parameter REGION=100K to the EXEC card.

IEHMOVE

19. IEHMOVE needs a special DD card for disk work space that looks like this: //SYSUT1   DD   UNIT=3330,SPACE=(TRK,30). More disk space is needed in the rare instances when the partitioned file you are working with has over 800 members.

20. When using IEHMOVE to move a partitioned file from disk onto tape (unloading) or from the tape back onto the disk (restoring), two DD cards are needed, one for disk and one for tape. They can have any DDnames. The one for the disk specifies a whole pack (UNIT, VOL, DISP). The DD

card for the tape specifies a new file on tape (DSN, UNIT, DISP=(NEW,KEEP))
when unloading the file to tape, and specifies an old file on tape (DSN,
UNIT, VOL, DISP=OLD) when restoring.

Unloading:

```
//DISK   DD   UNIT=3330,VOL=SER=D10040,DISP=OLD
//TAPE   DD   DSN=TAPE,UNIT=3400-3,DISP=(NEW,KEEP)
```

Restoring:

```
//DISK   DD   UNIT=3330,VOL=SER=D10040,DISP=OLD
//TAPE   DD   DSN=TAPE,UNIT=3400-3,VOL=SER=000040,DISP=OLD
```

21. IEHMOVE needs one control card, and COPY is the action word; PDS
gives the name of the partitioned file. FROM and TO specify the unit type
and volume serial numbers of the devices we are moving the file from and
to (when unloading, say TO=3400-3=SCRTCH).

Unloading:

```
//UNLDPDS    JOB     (accnt),NAME,MSGLEVEL=(1,1)
//STEP1      EXEC    PGM=IEHMOVE
//SYSPRINT   DD      SYSOUT=A
//SYSUT1     DD      UNIT=3330,SPACE=(TRK,30)
//DISK       DD      UNIT=3330,VOL=SER=D10040,DISP=OLD
//TAPE       DD      DSN=TAPE,UNIT=3400-3,DISP=(NEW,KEEP)
//SYSIN      DD      *
       COPY   PDS=PARTFILE,FROM=3330=D10040,TO=3400-3=SCRTCH,   C
              TODD=TAPE
/*
//
```

Restoring:

```
//RSTRPDS    JOB     (accnt),NAME,MSGLEVEL=(1,1)
//STEP1      EXEC    PGM=IEHMOVE
//SYSPRINT   DD      SYSOUT=A
//SYSUT1     DD      UNIT=3330,SPACE=(TRK,30)
//DISK       DD      UNIT=3330,VOL=SER=D10040,DISP=OLD
//TAPE       DD      DSN=TAPE,UNIT=3400-3,VOL=SER=000040,
//                   DISP=OLD
//SYSIN      DD      *
       COPY   PDS=PARTFILE,FROM=3400-3=000040,TO=3330=D10040, C
              FROMDD=TAPE
/*
//
```

IEHPROGM

22. IEHPROGM needs one DD card for the disk or drum you are working
with, specifying the whole pack (UNIT, VOL, DISP).

```
//DRUM   DD   UNIT=2305,VOL=SER=DD2305,DISP=OLD
```

23. Cataloging a file using IEHPROGM requires one control card, and CATLG
is the action word. The two parameters are DSNAME, giving the name of
the file, and VOL, giving the unit type and volume serial number of the
disk or tape the file is on.

```
//CATLG      JOB     (accnt),NAME,MSGLEVEL=(1,1)
//STEP1      EXEC    PGM=IEHPROGM
//SYSPRINT   DD      SYSOUT=A
//DRUM       DD      UNIT=2305,VOL=SER=DD2305,DISP=OLD
//SYSIN      DD      *
        CATLG  DSNAME=FILE=VOL=3330=D10040
/*
//
```

24. Uncataloging a file using IEHPROGM requires one control card, and
UNCATLG is the action word. The one parameter is DSNAME, giving the
name of the file to be uncataloged.

```
//UNCATLG    JOB     (accnt),NAME,MSGLEVEL=(1,1)
//STEP1      EXEC    PGM=IEHPROGM
//SYSPRINT   DD      SYSOUT=A
//DRUM       DD      UNIT=2305,VOL=SER=DD2305,DISP=OLD
//SYSIN      DD      *
      UNCATLG   DSNAME=FILE
/*
//
```

25. Renaming a file using IEHPROGM requires one control card, and RENAME
is the action word. The parameters are: DSNAME, giving the file's current
name; VOL, giving the unit type and volume serial number of the pack the
file is on; and NEWNAME, specifying the new name you want to give to
the file.

```
//RENAME     JOB     (accnt),NAME,MSGLEVEL=(1,1)
//STEP1      EXEC    PGM=IEHPROGM
//SYSPRINT   DD      SYSOUT=A
//DISK       DD      UNIT=3330,VOL=SER=D10040,DISP=OLD
//SYSIN      DD      *
      RENAME   DSNAME=LIB,VOL=3330=D10040,NEWNAME=LIBA
/*
//
```

26. Renaming a member of a partitioned file using IEHPROGM requires one
control card, and RENAME is the action word. The parameters are: DSNAME,
giving the name of the whole partitioned file; VOL, with the unit type and
volume serial number of the pack that the file is on; MEMBER, giving the
name of the member to be renamed; and NEWNAME specifies what you
want the member's new name to be.

```
//RENAMEM    JOB      (accnt),NAME,MSGLEVEL=(1,1)
//STEP1      EXEC     PGM=IEHPROGM
//SYSPRINT   DD       SYSOUT=A
//DISK       DD       UNIT=3330,VOL=SER=D10040,DISP=OLD
//SYSIN      DD       *
      RENAME   DSNAME=LIB,VOL=3330=D10040,MEMBER=MEM,       C
               NEWNAME=MEMA
/*
//
```

27. Scratching a file using IEHPROGM requires one control card, and SCRATCH
is the action word. The parameters are: DSNAME, naming the file you want
scratched; and VOL, giving the unit type and number of the pack it's on;
the parameter PURGE can be added if the file is to be scratched before its
expiration date.

```
//SRCHFILE   JOB      (accnt),NAME,MSGLEVEL=(1,1)
//STEP1      EXEC     PGM=IEHPROGM
//SYSPRINT   DD       SYSOUT=A
//DISK       DD       UNIT=3330,VOL=SER=D10040,DISP=OLD
//SYSIN      DD       *
      SCRATCH   DSNAME=SOMEFILE,VOL=3330=D10040
/*
//
```

28. Scratching a member of a partitioned file using IEHPROGM requires one
control card, and SCRATCH is the action word. The parameters are:
DSNAME, giving the name of the partitioned file; VOL, telling which unit
type and pack the file is on; and MEMBER, naming the member to be
scratched.

```
//SRCHMEM    JOB      (accnt),NAME,MSGLEVEL=(1,1)
//STEP1      EXEC     PGM=IEHPROGM
//SYSPRINT   DD       SYSOUT=A
//DISK       DD       UNIT=3330,VOL=SER=D10040,DISP=OLD
//SYSIN      DD       *
      SCRATCH   DSNAME=SOMEFILE,VOL=3330=D10040,            C
               MEMBER=SOMEMEM
/*
//
```

29. Scratching all the files on a disk pack using IEHPROGM requires one control card, and SCRATCH is the action word. The parameters are: VTOC,
with no equal sign; and VOL, giving the unit type and number of the pack
to be cleaned out; the parameter PURGE can be added to scratch files that
haven't yet expired.

```
//SRCHVTOC    JOB      (accnt),NAME,MSGLEVEL=(1,1)
//STEP1       EXEC     PGM=IEHPROGM
//SYSPRINT    DD       SYSOUT=A
//DISK        DD       UNIT=3330,VOL=SER=D10040,DISP=OLD
//SYSIN       DD       *
     SCRATCH    VTOC,VOL=3330=D10040,PURGE
/*
//
```

IEBPTPCH

30. IEBPTPCH needs two DD cards. The first, which must have the name
SYSUT1, describes the file you are printing from (often a cataloged, partitioned file on disk, needing DSN and DISP). The second DD card, which
must have the name SYSUT2, describes the printer (SYSOUT=A).

```
//SYSUT1   DD   DSNAME=SYS1.PROCLIB,DISP=SHR
//SYSUT2   DD   SYSOUT=A
```

31. Printing out individual members of a partitioned card image file using
IEBPTPCH requires three types of control cards. On the first card,
PRINT is the action word. Its three parameters are: TYPORG=PO, specifying the partitioned organization of the file; MAXNAME, giving the number of MEMBER cards that follow; and MAXFLDS, giving the number of
RECORD cards that follow. After that comes a pair of cards for every
member to be printed. MEMBER is the action word of the first card of
each pair; its parameter, NAME, names the member to be printed;
RECORD is the action word on the second card of each pair, and its
parameter, FIELD, gives the length of the record (usually FIELD=(80)).

```
//PRINTMEM    JOB      (accnt),NAME,MSGLEVEL=(1,1)
//STEP1       EXEC     PGM=IEBPTPCH
//SYSPRINT    DD       SYSOUT=A
//SYSUT1      DD       DSNAME=SYS1.PROCLIB,DISP=SHR
//SYSUT2      DD       SYSOUT=A
//SYSIN       DD       *
     PRINT      TYPORG=PO,MAXNAME=2,MAXFLDS=2
     MEMBER     NAME=WTR
     RECORD     FIELD=(80)
```

```
        MEMBER    NAME=RDR
        RECORD    FIELD=(80)
     /*
     //
```

32. Printing all the members of a partitioned card image file using IEBPTPCH requires two control cards. On the first card, PRINT is the action word. Its parameters are: TYPORG=PO, specifying partitioned organization; and MAXFLDS=1, saying that one RECORD card follows. RECORD is the action word of the second card, and its parameter is FIELD=(80), specifying the length of each record.

```
     //PRINTLIB    JOB     (accnt),NAME,MSGLEVEL=(1,1)
     //STEP1       EXEC    PGM=IEBPTPCH
     //SYSPRINT    DD      SYSOUT=A
     //SYSUT1      DD      DNS=SYS1.PROCLIB,DISP=SHR
     //SYSUT2      DD      SYSOUT=A
     //SYSIN       DD      *
            PRINT       TYPORG=PO,MAXFLDS=1
            RECORD    FIELD=(80)
     /*
     //
```

33. Punching out members of a partitioned card image file using IEBPTPCH involves the same DD cards and control cards used for printing the members, except that the SYSUT2 (output) DD card must refer to the card punch (SYSOUT=B), and the action word on the first control card is PUNCH.

34. To duplicate a card deck and put new sequence numbers in columns 73–80 of the new card deck using IEBPTPCH requires two DD cards. SYSUT1 is the name of the first, which refers to the old card deck (SYSUT1 DD *) and is followed by the deck itself; the name of the second DD card is SYSUT2, which refers to the card punch (SYSOUT=B). There are two control cards. PUNCH is the action word of the first, and its three parameters are: MAXFLDS=1; CDSEQ, to assign a beginning sequence number; and CDINCR, to assign an increment for following sequence numbers. The second control card is RECORD FIELD=(72), meaning you just want to duplicate the first 72 columns of the old card deck.

```
     //SEQCARDS    JOB     (accnt),NAME,MSGLEVEL=(1,1)
     //STEP1       EXEC    PGM=IEBPTPCH
     //SYSPRINT    DD      SYSOUT=A
     //SYSUT1      DD      *
```

[card deck to be resequenced goes here]

```
/*
//SYSUT2      DD       SYSOUT=B
//SYSIN       DD       *
       PUNCH     MAXFLDS=1,CDSEQ=0,CDINCR=100
       RECORD    FIELD=(72)
/*
//
```

IEBUPDTE

35. Modifying a partitioned card image file using IEBUPDTE requires two DD
cards, the first with the name SYSUT1, and the second with the name
SYSUT2, they both refer to the same file, the one being updated, which
is an old file on disk.

```
//SYSUT1   DD   DSNAME=SYS1.PROCLIB,DISP=OLD
//SYSUT2   DD   DSNAME=SYS1.PROCLIB,DISP=OLD
```

36. Adding a new member to a partitioned card image file using IEBUPDTE
requires three control cards, each with a ./ in columns 1 and 2. ADD is
the action word on the first. Its two parameters are: NAME, giving a name
to the new member; and LIST=ALL, saying you want the member printed
out. NUMBER is the action word on the second control card. Its parameters
are: NEW1, specifying the number the first card image is to have in columns 73–80; and INCR, saying how much larger than the one before it you
want the number in each card image to be. ENDUP is the action word of
the last card; it has no parameters. Between the NUMBER and ENDUP
cards are put the actual cards that are to become the new member.

```
//ADDMEM      JOB      (accnt),NAME,MSGLEVEL=(1,1)
//STEP1       EXEC     PGM=IEBUPDTE
//SYSPRINT    DD       SYSOUT=A
//SYSUT1      DD       DSN=SYS1.PROCLIB,DISP=OLD
//SYSUT2      DD       DSN=SYS1.PROCLIB,DISP=OLD
//SYSIN       DD       DATA
./   ADD      NAME=SAMPLE,LIST=ALL
./   NUMBER   NEW1=10,INCR=10
//STEP1       EXEC     PGM=EXAMPLE
//SYSPRINT    DD       SYSOUT=A
./   ENDUP
/*
//
```

37. When using IEBUPDTE, the SYSIN DD card should look like this—

```
//SYSIN  DD  DATA
```

—telling the system not to treat any JCL cards that follow as JCL cards until after the next /* card.

38. Replacing card images of a member in a partitioned card image file using IEBUPDTE requires two control cards, both with a ./ in columns 1 and 2. CHANGE is the action word on the first. Its two parameters are: NAME, giving the name of the member to be updated; and UPDATE=INPLACE, saying that the member can remain in the room it now occupies. ENDUP is the action word on the second control card, which has no parameters. In between them are put the replacement cards, each having in columns 73–80 the number that matches the card image it is to replace.

```
//UPDATE      JOB     (accnt),NAME,MSGLEVEL=(1,1)
//STEP1       EXEC    PGM=IEBUPDTE
//SYSPRINT    DD      SYSOUT=A
//SYSUT1      DD      DSN=SYS1.PROCLIB,DISP=OLD
//SYSUT2      DD      DSN=SYS1.PROCLIB,DISP=OLD
//SYSIN       DD      DATA
./   CHANGE   NAME=SAMPLE,UPDATE=INPLACE
//STEP2       EXEC    PGM=EXAMPLE2                        00000010
./   ENDUP
/*
//
```

39. Adding new card images to a member of a partitioned card image file using IEBUPDTE requires two control cards, both with a ./ in columns 1 and 2. CHANGE is the action word of the first. Its one parameter is NAME, giving the name of the member to be changed. ENDUP is the action word of the second control card, and it has no parameters. In between them are put the cards to be added, each having in columns 73–80 a number that indicates in between which card images it should be inserted.

```
//UPDATE2     JOB     (accnt),NAME,MSGLEVEL=(1,1)
//STEP1       EXEC    PGM=IEBUPDTE
//SYSPRINT    DD      SYSOUT=A
//SYSUT1      DD      DSN=SYS1.PROCLIB,DISP=OLD
//SYSUT2      DD      DSN=SYS1.PROCLIB,DISP=OLD
//SYSIN       DD      DATA
./   CHANGE   NAME=SAMPLE
//EXTRADD     DD      SYSOUT=A            00000015
./   ENDUP
/*
//
```

40. Deleting card images from a member of a partitioned card image file using IEBUPDTE requires two cards, both with a ./ in columns 1 and 2. The action word of the first is CHANGE, and its one parameter is NAME, giving the

name of the member to be changed; DELETE is the action word of the second control card, where SEQ1 gives the sequence number of the first card image to be deleted and SEQ2 gives the sequence number of the last card image to be deleted; the card images with those two sequence numbers and any in between are deleted. If only one card image is to be deleted, both SEQ1 and SEQ2 give the sequence number of the same card image, the one to be deleted.

```
//DELETE      JOB     (accnt),NAME,MSGLEVEL=(1,1)
//STEP1       EXEC    PGM=IEBUPDTE
//SYSPRINT    DD      SYSOUT=A
//SYSUT1      DD      DSN=SYS1.PROCLIB,DISP=OLD
//SYSUT2      DD      DSN=SYS1.PROCLIB,DISP=OLD
//SYSIN       DD      *
./  CHANGE    NAME=SAMPLE
./  DELETE    SEQ1=15,SEQ2=20
/*
//
```

41. When creating a new partitioned card image file using IEBUPDTE, the SYSUT1 DD card is left out; the SYSUT2 DD card is for a new file on disk (DSN, UNIT, DISP=(NEW,KEEP), SPACE (reserving space for the directory too), and usually VOL=SER to put it on a specific pack). The control cards are the same as for adding to an existing partitioned card image file, with the ADD and NUMBER control cards being repeated for and followed by each new member. The ADD control card gives each member a different name, and there is only one ENDUP card, which goes at the very end.

```
//NEWPDS      JOB     (accnt),NAME,MSGLEVEL=(1,1)
//STEP1       EXEC    PGM=IEBUPDTE
//SYSPRINT    DD      SYSOUT=A
//SYSUT1      DD      DSN=NEWFILE,UNIT=3330,VOL=SER=D10040,
//                    SPACE=(TRK,(50,,34))
//SYSIN       DD      DATA
./  ADD       NAME=SAMPLE,LIST=ALL
./  NUMBER    NEW1=10,INCR=10
//STEP1       EXEC    PGM=EXAMPLE
//SYSPRINT    DD      SYSOUT=A
./  ADD       NAME=SAMPLE2,LIST=ALL
./  NUMBER    NEW1=10,INCR=10
//STEP2       EXEC    PGM=EXAMPLE2
//SYSPRINT    DD      SYSOUT=A
./  ENDUP
/*
//
```

APPENDIX

WHICH UTILITY TO USE?

As you have noticed, there are many things that Utilities do. To help you zero in on the right Utility to use when you have a task to do, here is a list that tells which Utility does what. It is organized according to the types of devices and files that the Utilities do their work on. From here you can refer to the rules and examples that apply.

This is how we have divided the types of devices and files:
  I. Disks (and Drums)
     A. Whole disk packs.
     B. Partitioned files on disks.
     C. Individual members of a partitioned file.
     D. Sequential files on disks.
     E. The catalog.
 II. Tapes
     A. Files on tapes.
     B. Whole tapes.
III. Cards

Look for the type of device and file you are working with, and then under that for the action you want to do.

I. Disks (and Drums)
  A. Whole disk packs
     1. Listing the whole VTOC (seeing what files are on the disk pack and also the characteristics of each file).
        Utility: IEHLIST
        Control card: LISTVTOC   FORMAT,VOL=

Rules: 2, 1
Pages: 35–37

2. Printing the contents of individual tracks (exactly as it appears on the track).
   Utility: IEHDASDR
   Control card: DUMP   FROMDD=,TODD=,BEGIN=END=
   Rule: 10
   Pages: 48–50

3. Scratching all files off a disk pack (removing all entries from the VTOC).
   Utility: IEHPROGM
   Control card: SCRATCH   VTOC,VOL=,PURGE
   Rules: 29, 22
   Pages: 85–86

4. Scratching all the files with passed expiration dates.
   Utility: IEHPROGM
   Control card: SCRATCH   VTOC,VOL=   (without PURGE)
   Rules: 29, 22
   Pages: 85–86

5. Changing a disk pack's volume serial number (relabeling it).
   Utility: IEHDASDR
   Control card: LABEL   TODD=,NEWVOLID=
   Rule: 8
   Pages: 45–46

6. Initializing a new disk pack.
   Utility: IEHDASDR
   Control card: ANALYZE   TODD=(offline unit),VTOC=,EXTENT=,
                            NEWVOLID
   Rule: 6
   Pages: 41–43

7. Reinitializing an old disk pack.
   Utility: IEHDASDR
   Control card: ANALYZE TODD=(DD card),VTOC=,EXTENT-,NEWVOLID=,
                            PURGE=YES
   Rule: 7
   Pages: 44–45

8. Creating a backup tape by dumping the disk pack to tape.
   Utility: IEHDASDR
   Control card: DUMP   FROMDD=,TODD=
   Rule: 9
   Pages: 46–47

9. Restoring the contents of a disk pack from a backup tape.
   Utility: IEHDASDR

Control card: RESTORE   FROMDD=,TODD=,PURGE=YES
Rule: 11
Pages: 50–52

B. Partitioned files on disks

1. Listing out the names of its members.
   Utility: IEHLIST
   Control card: LIST PDS DSNAME,=VOL=
   Rules: 3, 1
   Page: 37

2. Printing out the contents of all of its members (card image only).
   Utility: IEBPTPCH
   Control cards: PRINT   TYPORG=PO,MAXFLDS=1
                    RECORD   FIELD=(80)
   Rules: 32, 30
   Pages: 89–93

3. Punching onto cards the contents of all of its members (card image only).
   Utility: IEBPTPCH
   Control cards: PUNCH   TYPORG=PO,MAXFLDS=1
                    RECORD   FIELD=(80)
   Rules: 33, 30
   Pages: 89–94

4. Adding a new member (card image only).
   Utility: IEBUPDTE
   Control cards: ./ ADD   NAME=,LIST=ALL
                   ./ NUMBER   NEW1=,INCR=
                        (new cards to become new member)
                   ./ ENDUP
   Rules: 36, 37, 35
   Pages: 99–104

5. Creating a whole new partitioned card image file, complete with new members.
   Utility: IEBUPDTE
   DD cards: SYSUT1—left out
                 SYSUT2—DSN, UNIT, DISP=(NEW KEEP),
                      SPACE (reserving directory space too),
                      (and usually VOL=SER also)
   Control cards: ./ ADD   NAME=, LIST=ALL
                   ./ NUMBER NEW1=, INCR=
                     (new cards to become new member)
                (the above is repeated for each new member)
                   ./ ENDUP

Rule: 41
Pages: 108–110

6. Unloading (backing up) the entire file onto a backup tape.
   Utility: IEHMOVE
   Control card: COPY   PDS=,FROM=,TO=,TODD=
   Rules: 20, 21, 19
   Pages: 71–75

7. Restoring the entire file from a backup tape.
   Utility: IEHMOVE
   Control card: COPY   PDS=,FROM=,FROMDD=,TO=
   Rules: 20, 21, 19
   Pages: 71–75

8. Copying the entire file to another disk pack.
   Utility: IEBCOPY
   Control card: COPY   INDD=,OUTDD=
   Rules: 15, 14
   Pages: 61–64

9. Compressing the file (moving its members to the front of the file,
   making the embedded free space available).
   Utility: IEBCOPY
   Control card: COPY   INDD=,OUTDD=   (both referring to the same file)
   Rules: 17, 14
   Pages: 66–67

10. Scratching the entire file (removing its entry from the VTOC and free-
    ing its space on the disk).
    Utility: IEHPROGM
    Control card: SCRATCH   DSNAME=,VOL=
    Rules: 27, 22
    Pages: 83–84

11. Renaming the file (giving it a new name).
    Utility: IEHPROGM
    Control card: RENAME   DSNAME=,VOL=,NEWNAME=
    Rules: 25, 22
    Page: 82

12. Cataloging the file (making an entry for it on the catalog).
    Utility: IEHPROGM
    Control card: CATLG   DSNAME=,VOL=
    Rules: 23, 22
    Page: 81

13. Uncataloging the file (taking its entry off the catalog).
    Utility: IEHPROGM
    Control card: UNCATLG   DSNAME=

Rules: 24, 22
Pages: 81–82

C. Individual members of a partitioned file

  1. Printing the member (listing it out—card image only).
    Utility: IEBPTPCH
    Control cards: PRINT   TYPORG=PO,MAXNAME=,MAXFLDS=
                    MEMBER NAME=
                    RECORD FIELD=(80)
    Rules: 31, 30
    Pages: 89–92

  2. Punching the member onto cards (card image only)
    Utility: IEBPTPCH
    Control cards: PUNCH   TYPORG=PO,MAXNAME=,MAXFLDS=
                    MEMBER NAME=
                    RECORD FIELD=(80)
    Rules: 33, 31, 30
    Pages: 89–94

  3. Replacing parts of the member with new card images (overlaying the old card images—card image only).
    Utility: IEBUPDTE
    Control cards: ./ CHANGE NAME=,UPDATE=INPLACE
                    (new cards with sequence numbers)
              ./ ENDUP
    Rules: 38, 37, 35
    Pages: 99–106

  4. Adding new card images to the member (in between or after the old card images, making the member larger—card image only).
    Utility: IEBUPDTE
    Control cards: ./ CHANGE NAME=
                    (new cards with sequence numbers)
              ./ ENDUP
    Rules: 39, 37, 35
    Pages: 99–106

  5. Deleting some card images from the member.
    Utility: IEBUPDTE
    Control cards: ./ CHANGE NAME=
                    ./ DELETE SEQ1=, SEQ2
    Rules: 40, 35
    Pages: 107–108

  6. Copying the member to another partitioned file.
    Utility: IEBCOPY
    Control cards: COPY   INDD=,OUTDD=
                    SELECT MEMBER=

Rules: 16, 14
Pages: 64–66

7. Scratching the member from the partitioned file (removing its entry from the directory and allowing its space to become available after the next compress).
   Utility: IEHPROGM
   Control card: SCRATCH   DSNAME=,VOL=,MEMBER=
   Rules: 28, 22
   Pages: 84–85

8. Renaming the member (giving the member a new name).
   Utility: IEHPROGM
   Control card: RENAME   DSNAME=,VOL=,MEMBER=
   Rules: 26, 22
   Pages: 82–83

D. Sequential files on disk packs
   1. Copying the disk file to tape.
      Utility: IEBGENER
      Control card: none
      DD cards: SYSUT1—old file on disk   (DSN,UNIT,VOL,DISP)
                   SYSUT2—new file on tape (DSN,UNIT,DISP=(NEW,KEEP),
                                       DCB=BLKSIZE=)

              SYSIN DD DUMMY
      Rules: 12, 13
      Pages: 55–59

   2. Copying the disk file to another disk.
      Utility: IEBGENER
      Control card: none
      DD cards: SYSUT1—old file on disk   (DSN,UNIT,VOL,DISP)
                   SYSUT2—new file on disk (DSN,UNIT,VOL,SPACE,
                                       DISP=(NEW,KEEP),
                                       DCB=BLKSIZE=)

              SYSIN DD DUMMY
      Rules: 12, 13
      Pages: 55–59

   3. Scratching the file off the disk.
      Utility: IEHPROGM
      Control card: SCRATCH   DSNAME=,VOL=
      Rules: 27, 22
      Pages: 83–84

   4. Printing the contents of the file.
      Utility: IEBGENER
      Control card: none

  DD cards: SYSUT1—old file on disk (DSN,UNIT,VOL,DISP)
       SYSUT2—SYSOUT=A,DCB=BLKSIZE=
       SYSIN DD DUMMY
  Rules: 12, 13
  Pages: 55–59

 5. Punching the contents of the file onto cards (for card image files only).
  Utility: IEBGENER
  Control card: none
  DD cards: SYSUT1—old file on disk (DSN,UNIT,VOL,DISP)
       SYSUT2—SYSOUT=B,DCB=BLKSIZE=80
       SYSIN DD DUMMY
  Rules: 12, 13
  Pages: 55–59

 6. Renaming the file (giving it a new name).
  Utility: IEHPROGM
  Control card: RENAME DSNAME=,VOL=,NEWNAME=
  Rules: 25, 22
  Page: 82

 7. Cataloging the file (putting an entry in the catalog pointing to it).
  Utility: IEHPROGM
  Control card: CATLG DSNAME=,VOL=
  Rules: 23, 22
  Page: 81

 8. Uncataloging the file (removing its entry from the catalog).
  Utility: IEHPROGM
  Control card: UNCATLG DSNAME=
  Rules: 24, 22
  Pages: 81–82

E. The catalog
 1. Listing the contents of the main catalog (to see what's on it).
  Utility: IEHLIST
  Control card: LISTCTLG
  Rules: 4, 1
  Page: 37

 2. Listing the contents of a secondary catalog.
  Utility: IEHLIST
  Control card: LISTCTLG CVOL=
  Rules: 5, 1
  Page: 38

 3. Adding to the catalog (cataloging a file).
  Utility: IEHPROGM
  Control card: CATLG DSNAME=,VOL=

Rules: 23, 22
Page: 81

4. Removing an entry from the catalog (uncataloging a file).
   Utility: IEHPROGM
   Control card: UNCATLG   DSNAME=
   Rules: 24, 22
   Pages: 81-82

II. Tapes
   A. Files on tapes
      1. Copying the file to another tape (duplicating it).
         Utility: IEBGENER
         Control card: none
         DD cards: SYSUT1—old file on tape   (DSN,UNIT,VOL,DISP)
                     SYSUT2—new file on tape (DSN,UNIT,DISP=(NEW,KEEP),
                                               DCB=BLKSIZE=)

                     SYSIN   DD DUMMY
         Rules: 12, 13
         Pages: 55-59

      2. Copying the file to a disk pack (creating a new sequential file on disk
         from the tape file).
         Utility: IEBGENER
         Control card: none
         DD cards: SYSUT1—old file on tape   (DSN,UNIT,VOL,DISP)
                     SYSUT2—new file on disk (DSN,UNIT,VOL,SPACE,
                                               DISP=(NEW,KEEP),
                                               DCB=BLKSIZE=)

                     SYSIN   DD DUMMY
         Rules: 12, 13
         Pages: 55-59

      3. Printing out what is on the tape file.
         Utility: IEBGENER
         Control card: none
         DD cards: SYSUT1—old file on tape (DSN,UNIT,VOL,DISP)
                     SYSUT2—SYSOUT=A,DCB=BLKSIZE=
                     SYSIN   DD DUMMY
         Rules: 12, 13
         Pages: 55-59

      4. Punching onto cards what is on the tape file (card image only).
         Utility: IEBGENER
         Control card: none
         DD cards: SYSUT1—old file on tape (DSN,UNIT,VOL,DISP)
                     SYSUT2—SYSOUT=B,DCB=BLKSIZE=
                     SYSIN   DD DUMMY

        Rules: 12, 13
        Pages: 55–59

5. Cataloging the file (making an entry for it on the catalog).
    Utility: IEHPROGM
    Control card: CATLG   DSNAME=,VOL=
    Rules: 23, 22
    Page: 81

6. Uncataloging the file (removing its entry from the catalog).
    Utility: IEHPROGM
    Control card: UNCATLG   DSNAME=
    Rules: 24, 22
    Pages: 81–82

B. Whole tapes

1. Dumping the contents of a disk pack to it (creating a backup tape).
    Utility: IEHDASDR
    Control card: DUMP   FROMDD=,TODD=
    Rule: 9
    Pages: 46–47

2. Restoring a disk pack from the tape (if it is a backup tape).
    Utility: IEHDASDR
    Control card: RESTORE   FROMDD=,TODD=
    Rule: 11
    Pages: 50–52

3. Unloading (backing up) a partitioned file onto a backup tape.
    Utility: IEHMOVE
    Control card: COPY   PDS=,FROM=,TO=,TODD=
    Rules: 20, 21, 19
    Pages: 71–75

4. Restoring a partitioned file from a backup tape.
    Utility: IEHMOVE
    Control card: COPY   PDS=,FROM=,FROMDD=,TO=
    Rules: 20, 21, 19
    Pages: 71–75

III. Cards

1. Duplicating the cards onto a new set of cards (all 80 columns).
    Utility: IEBGENER
    Control card: none
    DD cards: SYSUT1 DD * (followed by old cards)
                SYSUT2–SYSOUT=B,DCB=BLKSIZE=80
                SYSIN   DD DUMMY
    Rules: 12, 13
    Pages: 55–59

2. Duplicating just the first 72 columns of the cards onto a new set of

cards, putting new sequence numbers in columns 73–80.
    Utility: IEBPTPCH
    Control cards: PUNCH   MAXFLDS=1,CDSEQ=,CDINCR=
                     RECORD   FIELD=(72)
    Rules: 34, 30
    Pages: 94–96

3. Printing the contents of the cards (listing them out).
    Utility: IEBGENER
    Control card: none
    DD cards: SYSUT1 DD * (followed by the cards)
               SYSUT2–SYSOUT=A,DCB=BLKSIZE=80
               SYSIN   DD DUMMY
    Rules: 12, 13
    Pages: 55–59

4. Copying the cards onto a tape, creating a new file on tape.
    Utility: IEBGENER
    Control card: none
    DD cards: SYSUT1 DD * (followed by the cards)
               SYSUT2–new file on tape (DSN,UNIT,DISP=(NEW,KEEP),
                                 DCB=BLKSIZE=any multiple
                                 of 80)
               SYSIN   DD DUMMY
    Rules: 12, 13
    Pages: 55–59

5. Copying the cards onto a disk, creating a new sequential file on the
   disk.
    Utility: IEBGENER
    Control card: none
    DD cards: SYSUT1 DD * (followed by the cards)
               SYSUT2–new file on disk (DSN,UNIT,VOL,SPACE,DISP=
               SYSIN   DD DUMMY   (NEW,KEEP),DCB=BLKSIZE=
                                   any multiple of 80)
    Rules: 12, 13
    Pages: 55–59

ANSWERS

Chapter 1.   Overview of Computers, Files, Disk Packs, and Utilities

1. ADD, COMPARE, MOVE, and BRANCH
2. the processing unit
3. *a.* Main storage
   b. Program
4. *c*
5. Main storage (or instructions can also work on information in the processing unit itself)
6. Records
7. File
8. *a.* Reading, and input
   b. Writing, and output
9. Card reader/punch, printer, tape, disk
10. *a.* 11
    b. 20
    c. The very top and very bottom surfaces
11. Tracks
12. *a.* A volume serial number and a volume table of contents
    b. Initializing
13. In the volume table of contents of the disk pack
14. *a.* A directory
    b. The names of the members in the partitioned file
15. *a.* No
    b. The file has to be compressed
16. Restoring
17. Card images
18. An offline device
19. A volume table of contents of a disk pack, a directory of a partitioned file, and the catalog

20. Disk
21. *a.* Add entries (catalog files), and remove entries (uncatalog files)
    b. Remove entries (scratch files), and rename entries (rename files)
    c. Remove entries (scratch members), and rename entries (rename members)
22. *Print/Punch*
23. *a.* Partitioned
    b. Sequential
    c. Partitioned
24. Binary
25. 8
26. 1000 (1024, to be exact)
27. 800 bytes
28. The size of the program (the instructions themselves), and the space needed for the buffers for the file with the largest blocks.

Chapter 2. JCL

1. IE
2. //
3. JOB, EXEC, and DD
4. The EXEC card, PGM=
5. *a.* REGION=
   b. REGION=50K
   c. It goes on the EXEC card (and also on the JOB card)
6. Card reader/punch, printer, tape, and disk
7. Data definition
8. *a.* In column 3, right after the //
   b. From 1 to 8 characters (the first must be a letter)
9. Output file
10. SYSOUT=A
11. SYSOUT=B
12. DSNAME, UNIT, VOL=SER, DISP, LABEL, and SPACE
13. *a.* Tape drive
    b. Disk drive
14. *a.* DISP=(NEW,KEEP)
    b. DISP=(OLD,DELETE)
    c. DISP=(SHR,KEEP) or just DISP=SHR
15. Yes
16. *c*
17. SER
18. DSN

19. *a.* LABEL=(1,SL) or leave out the LABEL parameter
    b. LABEL=(2,NL)
20. *a.* SPACE=(CYL,30)
    b. SPACE=(TRK,(20.10))
21. *a.* LABEL=(1,SL)
    b. DISP=(NEW,DELETE)
22. *a.* No
    b. No
    c. Yes
    d. No
23. *a.* UNIT and VOL=SER
    b. From the catalog
24. It just puts the file on a scratch pack
25. *a.* DSN, UNIT, VOL=SER, DISP=OLD (or SHR)
    b. DSN, DISP=OLD (or SHR)
    c. DSN, UNIT, DISP=(NEW,KEEP), SPACE, (and optionally VOL=SER)
    d. UNIT, SPACE
    e. UNIT, VOL=SER, DISP=OLD (or SHR)
26. LABEL (only for specially labeled tapes)
    and SPACE (only for new files on disk)

Chapter 3.   The Control Card

1. ```
   //JOBNAME   JOB     (accnt),NAME,MSGLEVEL=(1,1)
   //STEP1        EXEC  PGM=(name of Utility)
   //SYSPRINT  DD      SYSOUT=A
   ```
2. The name of the program you want to use, after the word PGM on the
   EXEC card.
3. `//STEP1   EXEC   PGM=IEHLIST`
4. *a.* SYSOUT=A
   b. The printer
   c. Every Utility needs a place to put its printed output to at least tell
      you what it has done, or if there are errors with your control card.
5. The DD cards, and the control card(s).
6. The control card.
7. `//SYSIN DD *`
8. No
9. *a.* The action word
   b. No
10. Parameters
11. 34
12. IEBGENER
   ```

13. It includes the unit type instead of the letters SER (example: VOL=3330=
    D10040 instead of VOL=SER=D10040)
14. No
15. *a.* A blank
    b. No
16. *a.* Column 16
    b. No

Chapter 4.   IEHLIST

1. *a.* No
   b. UNIT, VOL=SER, DISP=OLD
   c. Any DD name
2. *a.* LISTVTOC
   b. LISTPDS
   c. LISTCTLG
3. VOL
4. *a.* LISTVTOC   FORMAT,VOL=3330=D10030
   b. LISTPDS   DSNAME=PARTFILE,VOL=3330=D10040
   c. LISTCTLG
   d. LISTCTLG   CVOL=3330=D10030
5. Control *Vol*ume
6. (We'll use the DD name DISK, but any DD name is permissible.)
   a. //DISK DD UNIT=3330,VOL=SER=D10020,DISP=OLD
   b. //DISK DD UNIT=3330,VOL=SER=D10020,DISP=OLD
   c. //DISK DD UNIT=3330,VOL=SER=D10040,DISP=OLD
   d. //DISK DD UNIT=3330,VOL=SER=D10020,DISP=OLD

Chapter 5.   IEHDASDR

1. An offline disk drive
2. No DD card
3. Volume serial number and a volume table of contents
4. ANALYZE
5. The unit number of the offline disk drive where the disk to be initialized
   is
6. VTOC=1,EXTENT=10
7. NEWVOLID
8. PASSES=4
9. To check for possible bad spots on the disk pack
10. No
11. Yes
12. The DDname of the DD card for the disk pack being reinitialized

13.   ANALYZE
14.   PURGE=YES
      It means that if there are any files on the disk pack, they can be erased
      while checking the pack for bad spots (without PURGE=YES, IEHDASDR
      will stop upon finding such a file)
15.   *a.* LABEL
      b. TODD and NEWVOLID
16.   (Again we'll use an arbitrary DDname of DISK.)
      a. LABEL   TODD=DISK,NEWVOLID=D10025
      b. //DISK DD UNIT=3330,VOL=SER=D10020,DISP=OLD
17.   *a.* DUMP
      b. DUMP
      c. RESTORE
18.   FROMDD and TODD
19.   The file of the SYSPRINT DD card
20.   BEGIN=00080001,END=001E000B
21.   *a.* DISP=(NEW,KEEP)
      b. DISP=OLD
22.   *a.* DUMP   FROMDD=DISK,TODD=TAPE
      b. RESTORE   FROMDD=TAPE, TODD=DISK
23.   (Using DISK as an arbitrary DD name)
      a. //DISK   DD   UNIT=3330,VOL=SER=D10020,DISP=OLD
      b. //DISK   DD   UNIT=3330,VOL=SER=D10020,DISP=OLD
      c. //DISK   DD   UNIT=3330,VOL=SER=D10020,DISP=OLD
      d. //DISK   DD   UNIT=3330,VOL=SER=D10020,DISP=OLD
24.   *a.* //TAPE   DD   DSN=TAPE,UNIT=3400-3,VOL=SER=002000,
      //   DISP=(NEW,KEEP)
      b. //TAPE   DD   DSN=TAPE,UNIT=3400-3,VOL=SER=002000,DISP=OLD
25.   (Assuming the DD name of the disk is DISK)
      DUMP   FROMDD=DISK,TODD=SYSPRINT,BEGIN=00320005,END=00320005
26.   C8

Chapter 6.   IEBGENER

1.   Sequential files
2.   *a.* SYSUT1
     b. SYSUT2
3.   No
4.   //SYSIN DD DUMMY
5.   Card reader, tape, and disk
6.   DSN, UNIT, VOL=SER, DISP
7.   *a.* //SYSUT1   DD   *
     b. //SYSUT1   DD   DSN=SEQFILE,UNIT=3330,VOL=SER=D10020,DISP=OLD

   c. //SYSUT1   DD   DSN=TAPEFILE,VOL=SER=002000,UNIT=3400-3,
   //   DISP=OLD
   d. //SYSUT1   DD   DSN=LIBFILE(MEM1),UNIT=3330,VOL=SER=D10025,
   //   DISP=OLD
   (in *b, c,* and *d,* the DISP parameter could also be DISP=SHR)
8. DCB=BLKSIZE=
9. The blocksize must be a multiple of the record size
10. No
11. *a.* Yes
    b. Yes
       (Except for variable size records and blocks, which we didn't discuss
       because they are rare)
12. Card punch, printer, tapes, and disks
13. *a.* //SYSUT2   DD   SYSOUT=A,DCB=BLKSIZE=80
    b. //SYSUT2   DD   SYSOUT=B,DCB=BLKSIZE=80
14. DISP=(NEW,KEEP)
15. *a.* //SYSUT2   DD   DSN=FILE,UNIT=3400-3,DISP=(NEW,KEEP),
    //   DCB=BLKSIZE=800
    b. //SYSUT2   DD   DSN=FILE,UNIT=3330,VOL=SER=D10020,
    //   DISP=NEW,KEEP),SPACE=(CYL,40),DCB=BLKSIZE=800

Chapter 7. IEBCOPY

1. Partitioned files
2. *a.* Work space for IEBCOPY
   b. SYSUT3 and SYSUT4
   c. UNIT and SPACE
3. //SYSUT3   DD   UNIT=3330,SPACE=(TRK,10)
   //SYSUT4   DD   UNIT=3330,SPACE=(TRK,10)
4. *a.* Two
   b. Any DD names you choose
5. *a.* DSN, UNIT, VOL=SER, DISP
   b. DSN, DISP
   c. DISP=OLD or DISP=SHR
6. *a.* DSN, UNIT, VOL=SER, DISP, SPACE
   b. DISP=(NEW,KEEP)
   c. SPACE=(TRK,(100,,30))
   d. It's used to reserve space for the directory
7. (The DDnames FROMDISK and TODISK are arbitrary.)
   //FROMDISK   DD   DSN=PARTFILE,UNIT=3330,VOL=SER=D10020,
   //   DISP=OLD
   //TODISK   DD   DSN=PARTFILE,UNIT=3330,VOL=SER=D10010,
   //   DISP=(NEW,KEEP),SPACE=(TRK,(50,,40))

8. *a.* COPY
   b. INDD and OUTDD
   c. COPY   INDD=OLDDISK,OUTDD=NEWDISK
9. *a.* DISP=OLD
   b. DISP=OLD
   c. DSN, UNIT, VOL=SER, DISP
10. *a.* 2
    b. COPY
    c. INDD and OUTDD
    d. SELECT and EXCLUDE
    e. MEMBER=
11. *a.* SELECT
    b. EXCLUDE
12. COPY   INDD=FROMDISK,OUTDD=TODISK
    SELECT   MEMBER=(MEM1,MEM2)
13. One
14. *a.* COPY
    b. INDD and OUTDD
    c. They are the same DD card
15. REGION=100K

Chapter 8.   IEHMOVE

1. Partitioned file
2. Unloading a file
3. *a.* SYSUT1
   b. UNIT and SPACE
   c. 50 tracks
   d. //SYSUT1   DD   UNIT=3330,SPACE=(TRK,50)
4. *a.* Tape and disk
   b. Tape and disk
5. *a.* Disk is input; tape is output
   b. Tape is input; disk is output
6. *a.* 2
   b. They can have any DDnames
7. Yes
8. UNIT, VOL=SER, and DISP=OLD
9. *a.* //DISK   DD   UNIT=3330,VOL=SER=D10020,DISP=OLD
   b. //DISK   DD   UNIT=3330,VOL=SER=D10020,DISP=OLD
   (The DDname of DISK is arbitrary; any DDname can be used.)
10. *a.* When unloading
    b. When restoring
11. *a.* DISP=(NEW,KEEP)

       b. DISP=SHR (or OLD)

12. *a.* No

       b. We don't really care what output tape is used, and if we leave out the VOL=SER parameter, the system has a scratch tape mounted.

       c. We restore from a specific tape, in which case we must specify a volume serial number.

13. *a.* DSN, UNIT, and DISP

       b. DSN=TAPE,UNIT=3400-3,DISP=(NEW,KEEP)

         (The DSN of TAPE is arbitrary; any name can be used).

14. *a.* DSN, UNIT, VOL=SER, DISP

       b. DSN=TAPE,UNIT=3400-3,VOL=SER=000020,DISP=OLD

15. *a.* No

       b. Either scratch or rename the old disk file (and make sure there's enough space on the disk left for the restored file).

16. One

17. COPY

18. PDS

19. TO and FROM

20. *a.* FROM

       b. TO

21. *a.* PDS=FILE1

       b. FROM=3330=D10025

       c. TO=3400-3=SCRTCH

22. *a.* PDS=FILE1

       b. FROM=3400-3=000025

       c. TO=3330=D10025

23. *b*

24. *b*

25. *a.* TODD

       b. FROMDD

26. *a.* FROMDD=TAPE

       b. TODD=TAPE

27. *a.* COPY   PDS=PARTFILE,FROM=3330=D10080,TO=3400-3=SCRTCH,   C
                TODD=TAPE

       b. COPY   PDS=PARTFILE,FROM=3400-3=000085,TO=3330=D10080,   C
                FROMDD=TAPE

Chapter 9. IEHPROGM

1. *a.* Add entries (catalog files) and remove entries (uncatalog files)

       b. Remove entries (scratch files) and rename entries (rename files)

       c. Remove entries (scratch members) and rename entries (rename members)

2.   *a.* Any DDname you choose
     b. UNIT, VOL=SER, and DISP=OLD
     c. Because IEHPROGM often works with the whole pack (such as when it works with the VTOC of a disk)
3.   *a.* RENAME
     b. UNCATLG
     c. SCRATCH
     d. CATLG
4.   *a.* DSNAME
     b. DSNAME, VOL
     c. DSNAME, VOL, NEWNAME
     d. DSNAME, VOL, MEMBER, NEWNAME
5. An entry on the catalog includes the volume serial number of the tape or disk that holds the file. Therefore, to create an entry in the catalog, you must supply this information. But this information is not needed to remove the entry from the catalog—all that is necessary is that the entry be located, in order that it be deleted, and the DSname is enough information for that.
6.   *a.* CATLG   DSNAME=FILEONE,VOL=3400-3=002000
     b. UNCATLG DSNAME=FILEONE
     c. RENAME   DSNAME=DSKFILE1,VOL=3330=D10020,NEWNAME-DSKFILE2
     d. RENAME   DSNAME=PARTFILE,VOL=3330=D10020,MEMBER=OLD,   C
                         NEWNAME=NEW
7.   *a.* The files on disk and tape
     b. The file on disk
     c. The file on disk
8.   *a.* NEWNAME
     b. MEMBER
9. The whole file would be renamed
10. The whole file would be scratched (something to be avoided)
11.   *a.* D10040
     b. D10020
12. PURGE
13. VTOC
14. Yes—PURGE only refers to the whole file, not to individual members
15.   *a.* VOL
     b. DSNAME
16.   *a.* SCRATCH DSNAME=FILEA,VOL=3330=D10010
     b. SCRATCH DSNAME=FILEA,VOL=3330=D10010,PURGE
     c. SCRATCH DSNAME=FILEB,VOL=3330=D10005,MEMBER=MEMA
     d. SCRATCH VTOC,VOL=3330=D10005
     e. SCRATCH VTOC,VOL=3330=D10005,PURGE

Chapter 10.   IEBPTPCH

1. *Print/Punch*
2. SYSUT1 and SYSUT2
3. *a.* //SYSUT2   DD   SYSOUT=A
   b. //SYSUT2   DD   SYSOUT=B
4. *a.* //SYSUT1   DD   DSN=FILE,UNIT=3330,VOL=SER=D10010,DISP=SHR
   b. //SYSUT1   DD   DSN=FILE2,DISP=SHR
5. PRINT, MEMBER, and RECORD
6. *a.* NAME=
   b. FIELD=
7. RECORD   FIELD=(80)
8. *a.* MAXNAME
   b. MAXFLDS
9. The MEMBER card must come first
10. MEMBER   NAME=MEMA
    RECORD   FIELD=(80)
11. TYPORG=PO
12. PRINT   TYPORG=PO,MAXNAME=1,MAXFLDS=1
    MEMBER   NAME=MEMB
    RECORD   FIELD=(80)
13. The MEMBER control card
14. MAXNAME
15. PRINT   TYPORG=PO,MAXFLDS=1
    RECORD   FIELD=(80)
16. *a.* The PRINT control card
    b. The action word PRINT
    c. No
17. SYSOUT=B
18. Columns 73–80
19. IEBGENER
20. *a.* *
    b. The card deck to be duplicated
    c. SYSOUT=B
21. *a.* PUNCH and RECORD
    b. RECORD   FIELD=(72)
    c. We are only duplicating the first 72 columns of the card instead of all
        80 columns, so we say FIELD=(72) as opposed to FIELD=(80)
22. MAXFLDS
23. CDSEQ and CDINCR
24. *a.* CDSEQ=0,CDINCR=10
    b. PUNCH   MAXFLDS=1,CDSEQ=0,CDINCR=10
        RECORD   FIELD=(72)

Chapter 11.   IEBUPDTE

1. *b* and *c* (In other words, it *can't* be sequential and *can't* contain translated programs; it *must* be a partitioned, card image file.)
2. *a.* SYSUT1 and SYSUT2
   b. One
3. DISP=OLD
4. *a.* DSN, UNIT, VOL=SER
   b. DSN
5. The DDnames themselves, SYSUT1 as opposed to SYSUT2—the rest of the cards are identical
6. *a.* ./
   b. Yes
7. ADD, CHANGE, NUMBER, DELETE, and ENDUP
8. No—they are mutually exclusive operations
9. *a.* The ENDUP control card
   b. It has no parameters
10. ADD, NUMBER, and ENDUP
11. To add sequence numbers to columns 73-80 of the card images
12. The ADD control card must precede the NUMBER control card
13. NAME=
14. LIST=ALL
15. The ADD control card
16. *a.* NEW1 and INCR
    b. NEW1=100,INCR=100
17. The card images would not have sequence numbers in columns 73-80 (so they could not be changed using IEBUPDTE)
18. ./   ADD   NAME=NEWMEM,LIST=ALL
    ./   NUMBER   NEW1=100,INCR=100
    ./   ENDUP
19. Between the NUMBER and ENDUP control cards
20. Yes
21. //SYSIN   DD   DATA
22. /*
23. The JCL cards that follow your job would be gobbled up as input data to your job, and those jobs would not be run—this would continue until the first /* is encountered.
24. CHANGE
25. NAME=
26. Sequence numbers
27. Sequence numbers
28. UPDATE=INPLACE
29. Just NAME=

30. *a.* ./   CHANGE   NAME=MEM,UPDATE=INPLACE
       ./   ENDUP
    b. ./   CHANGE   NAME=MEM
       ./   ENDUP
31. Between the CHANGE and ENDUP control cards
32. CHANGE and DELETE
33. The name of the member to be changed
34. SEQ1 and SEQ2
35. *a.* SEQ1=500,SEQ2=900
    b. SEQ1=30,SEQ2=30
36. No
37. ./   CHANGE NAME=MEM1
    ./   DELETE SEQ1=350,SEQ2=450
38. The SYSUT1 DD card
39. SYSUT2
40. *b*
41. DISP=(NEW,KEEP)
42. SPACE=(TRK,(105,,50))
43. ADD and NUMBER
44. The ADD control card
45. *a.* 10
    b. 1
    c. At the very end of all the control cards and cards that are to become
       the new members

Chapter 12.   Having Utilities Do More Than One Thing at a Time

1. *a.* Yes
   b. (Using arbitrary DDnames of DISK1 and DISK2)
      //DISK1   DD   UNIT=3330,VOL=SER=D10040,DISP=OLD
      //DISK2   DD   UNIT=3330,VOL=SER=D10020,DISP=OLD
         LISTCTLG
         LISTCTLG   CVOL=3330=D10020
2. *a.* Yes
   b. COPY   INDD=FILE1,OUTDD=FILE1
      COPY   INDD=FILE2,OUTDD=FILE2
      COPY   INDD=FILE3,OUTDD=FILE3
3. *a.* Yes
   b. Yes
   c. IEHDASDR would do the first six at the same time; when they were
      done, it would do the last one
4. Yes

5. *a.* UNCATLG DSNAME=FILE
    UNCATLG DSNAME=DISKFILE
    UNCATLG DSNAME=TAPEFILE
    UNCATLG DSNAME=LIBFILE
  b. One
  c. Because the DD card refers to the catalog, not to the files we are un-cataloging

6. No, because they are done by two different Utilities: IEHPROGM and IEHLIST

7. *a.* Ten, one for each pack
  b. One, for that one pack, because the DD card for IEHPROGM refers to the whole pack, with no DSNAME parameter

8. *a.* Yes
  b. Six DD cards, one for each file, each with a different DDname

9. *a.* No
  b. Because IEBPTPCH can work with only one file at a time (SYSUT1 can only be one file)

10. *a.* No
  b. Because IEBUPDTE also can work with only one file at a time (again, SYSUT1 can only be one file)
  c. Yes
  d. ./ CHANGE NAME=MEM1
      (addition card with sequence number goes here)
    ./ CHANGE NAME=MEM2
      (addition with sequence number)
    ./ ENDUP
(Notice only one ENDUP control card at the very end)

11. They all require SYSUT1 and SYSUT2 DD cards, and so can work with only one file at a time.

12. *a.* No
  b. Run two different jobs each using IEBGENER at the same time

INDEX